IMAGES
of America

CUMBERLAND TOWNSHIP AND CARMICHAELS

On the Cover: The Tri-State Fox Hunters Association was comprised of not only farmers but also businessmen. Sometimes, even women would join the hunt. Foxhunts would last for four days. The headquarters for the foxhunters was the Home Hotel. This November 1, 1900, photograph shows a group of foxhunters in front of the Flenniken Livery Stable. J.C. Fremont Flenniken is standing in the middle holding the fox. (Courtesy of the Greene County Historical Society and Museum.)

IMAGES
of America

CUMBERLAND TOWNSHIP AND CARMICHAELS

Shelley McMinn Anderson

ARCADIA
PUBLISHING

ISBN 978-1-4671-2457-7

Published by Arcadia Publishing
Charleston, South Carolina

Printed in the United States of America

Library of Congress Control Number: 2016943673

For all general information, please contact Arcadia Publishing:
Telephone 843-853-2070
Fax 843-853-0044
E-mail sales@arcadiapublishing.com
For customer service and orders:
Toll-Free 1-888-313-2665

Visit us on the Internet at www.arcadiapublishing.com

To our ancestors, whose steadfast determination created one of the most charming towns in America.

Contents

Acknowledgments

This book was made possible thanks to the individuals and organizations that have shared their photographs, memories, and family records with the Carmichaels Area Historical Society, making valuable chapters of our area's history available to the public. Collecting images, digitizing, and properly labeling those images requires time, research, and lots of help. In searching for images of Cumberland Township and Carmichaels, it was disappointing to find that large portions of our photographic history have been lost.

There are so many people to thank that I could not possibly name them all, so I'll say thank you to everyone who helped, not only for locating and providing photographs but also identifying dates, names, places, and events. A special thank-you is owed to my cousin Carole Gideon; for a year, she went everywhere with me to aid in the search for and digitalization of images. I would like to thank my family for listening to me talk constantly about the history of the town. Thanks also go to Brenda and all the volunteers and staff at the Cornerstone Genealogy Society, Eben and Alexandra at the Greene County Historical Society and Museum, and the staff of the Flenniken Memorial Library.

I love researching and learning about early settlers, and finding pictures of them or their places of business or homes makes them come alive. They are no longer just a name on a piece of paper. Being able to share a part of this history through this book is wonderful. Being able to further share the full story behind a picture through the Carmichaels Area Historical Society is something that I still greatly enjoy.

INTRODUCTION

Carmichaels was named in honor of pioneer settler James Carmichael. He owned the land where the present-day town is located, and called the area Lisbon. Although trappers and traders had been in the area for many years, the largest group of pioneers settled in the summer of 1767 on the banks of Muddy Creek in what became known as Old Town, making it one of the earliest settlements in Western Pennsylvania. The people of the Carmichaels area are extremely proud of their hard work and fortitude.

Knowledge of the existence of coal in Western Pennsylvania was known before the Revolutionary War; however, it was not until the latter part of the 1800s that the first coal was dug, carted, and wheeled out by hand. There have been more than half a dozen local mines, drawing immigrants from all over Europe. These workers brought not only their families but also their customs to the Carmichaels area, creating a unique culture. Coal mining became the area's main industry and employer. In 1942, due to the increased demands for coal for electrical power, fuel, and steel production, a local chapter of the United Mine Workers Association was established. The King Coal Association was formed in Carmichaels to promote the bituminous coal industry. The first annual Pennsylvania Bituminous Coal Show was held in 1954 and continues today.

Starting in 1852, Carmichaels hosted a weeklong fair that was the highlight of rural living. The fair, held annually until around 1935, had an average attendance of around 5,000 each year. Farmers proudly showed their livestock. Exhibit halls included farm products and goods. Horse racing, baseball games, and high-class musical entertainment brought the community together. For more than 80 years, the Carmichaels Fair drew in residents and visitors from the tristate area, making it a significant contributor to the local economy and substantial part of Carmichaels's history.

Although a covered bridge has stood across Muddy Creek since the late 1700s, the current covered bridge was built in 1889. This still-used picturesque bridge separates Old Town from Carmichaels, which at one time was known as New Town, and is a popular attraction at the annual Covered Bridge Festival held every third weekend of September. Due to courting and marriage proposals taking place in this secluded structure, it became known as the "kissing bridge." It is listed in the National Register of Historic Places and is a treasured piece of Carmichaels's Americana, past and present.

The Greene Academy in Carmichaels was the first school of higher learning west of the Allegheny Mountains and was chartered in 1810. The stone side of the building, constructed in 1790, was originally an Episcopal church. In 1810, with state funding from the Pennsylvania legislature and the understanding that the money was to be used for building purposes, the brick side of the building was added. The brick portion of the building was to be used, in part, for "teaching poor children gratis under the law of 1809." The Greene Academy was the leading institution for education through the Civil War era, training many future school teachers and notable persons, including Dr. Miller, president of Waynesburg College; Albert B. Cummins, who became a US senator and governor of Iowa; and Thomas S. Crago, who became a US congressman. After the Civil War, the school was used as a grade school. The academy closed in 1893 as other grade schools were built throughout the area. In fact, there were more than a dozen one-room schools in the Carmichaels area from the late 1700s until 1960. Carmichaels Area High School broke ground in 1928 and is in the middle of a renovation project. Waynesburg College, now University, took over as the area's leader in higher education. Multiple generations have attended the same schools. Community members take pride in this rich history, and in 1970, they renovated the original academy. Today, the Greene Academy of Art provides for the building's care and maintenance and holds arts classes for all ages. It is also the home for the Carmichaels Area Historical Society. While the number of students touched by these organizations and their descendants is unknown, these schools have played a crucial role in Carmichaels's common heritage. The Greene Academy is listed in the National Register of Historic Places.

Veterans from Carmichaels have served in every war from the Revolutionary War to present-day military actions. Memorial Day and Veterans Day are of utmost importance and are sacred occasions to the citizens of Carmichaels. Ceremonies are held annually in the town square, paying tribute to loved ones who have served and sacrificed for their country. Carmichaels hosts both the American Legion Post No. 400 and Veterans of Foreign Wars Post No. 3491.

One

Organizations and Recreation

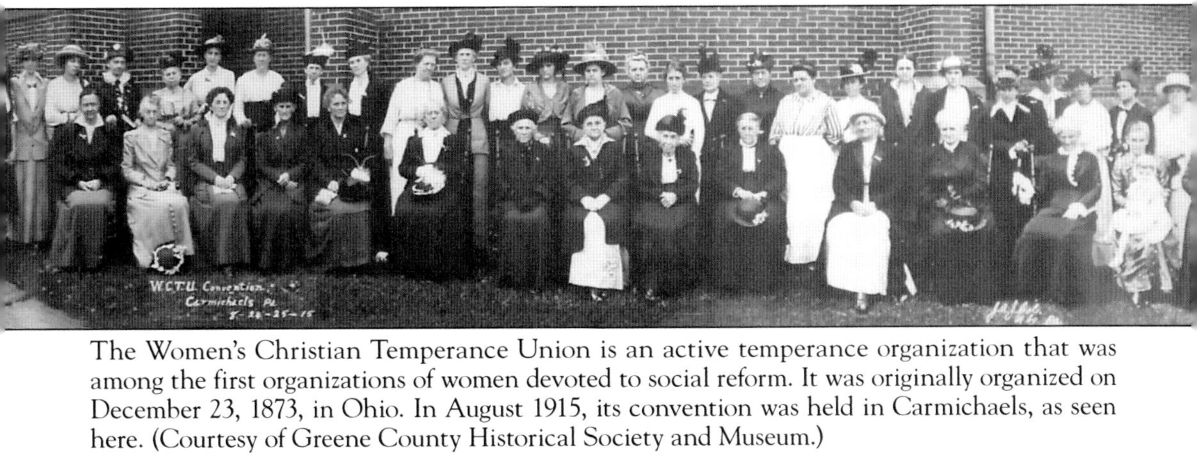

The Women's Christian Temperance Union is an active temperance organization that was among the first organizations of women devoted to social reform. It was originally organized on December 23, 1873, in Ohio. In August 1915, its convention was held in Carmichaels, as seen here. (Courtesy of Greene County Historical Society and Museum.)

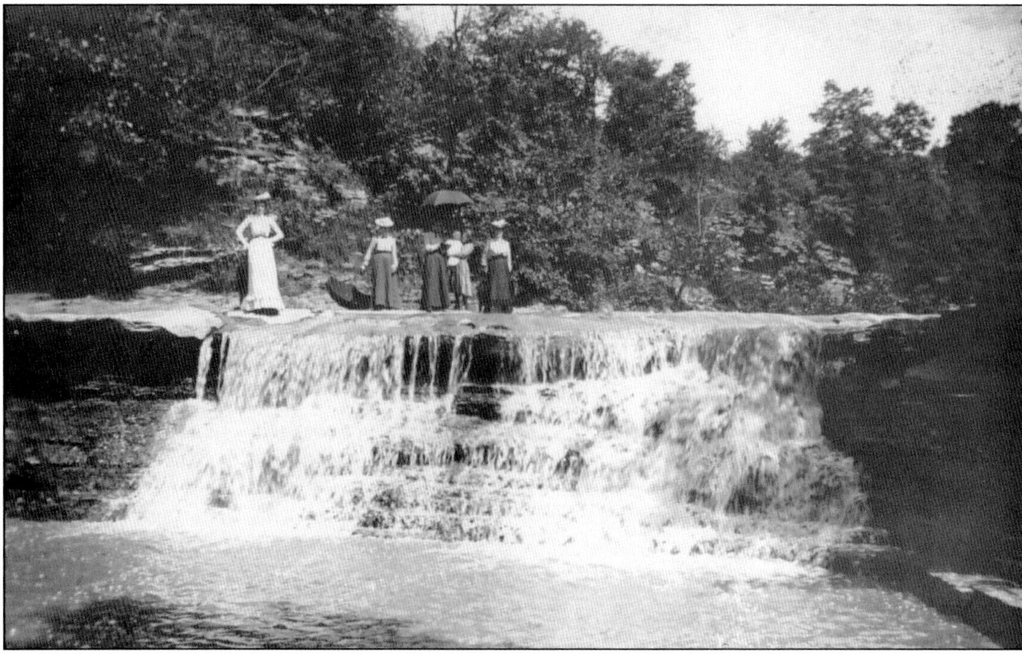

Pictured standing very close to the falls, these women are dressed in their Sunday best. On warm summer days, especially on Sundays, the townsfolk would dress in their finest clothing, gather at the public square, and walk to the Laurel and Sand Rocks at the falls to spend the afternoon. (Courtesy of Carole Gideon.)

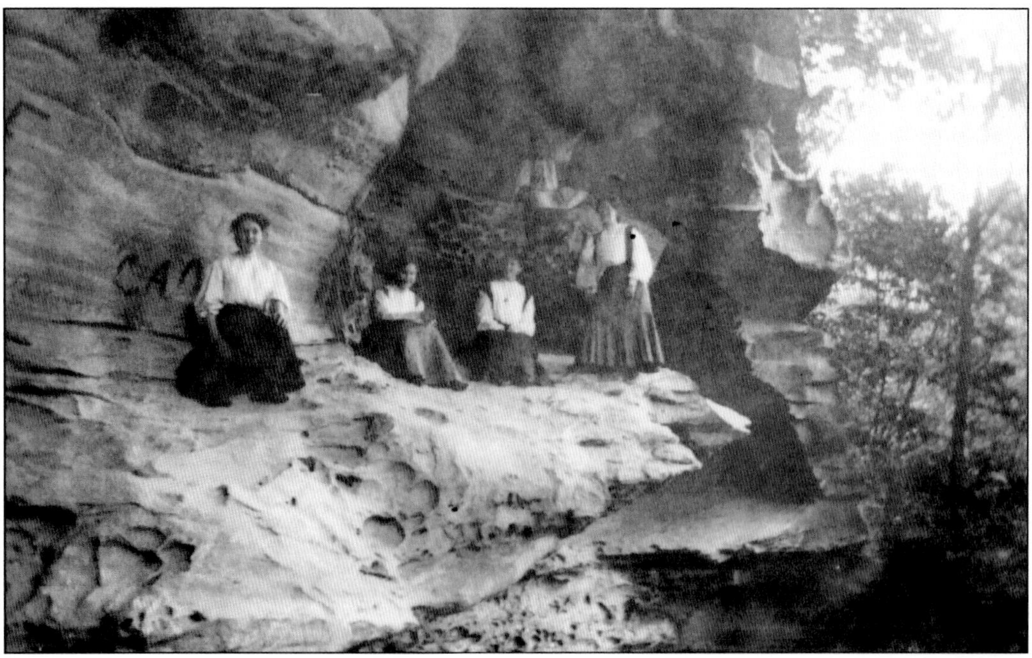

A group of unidentified young ladies is posing for a photograph at Sand Rock, just above the falls at Laurel Point. The Sand Rock was once a temporary retreat for Indians in the late 1700s. John Flenniken and his brother James claimed this area at Sand Rock and over 10,000 acres of land in Cumberland Township. (Courtesy of Carole Gideon.)

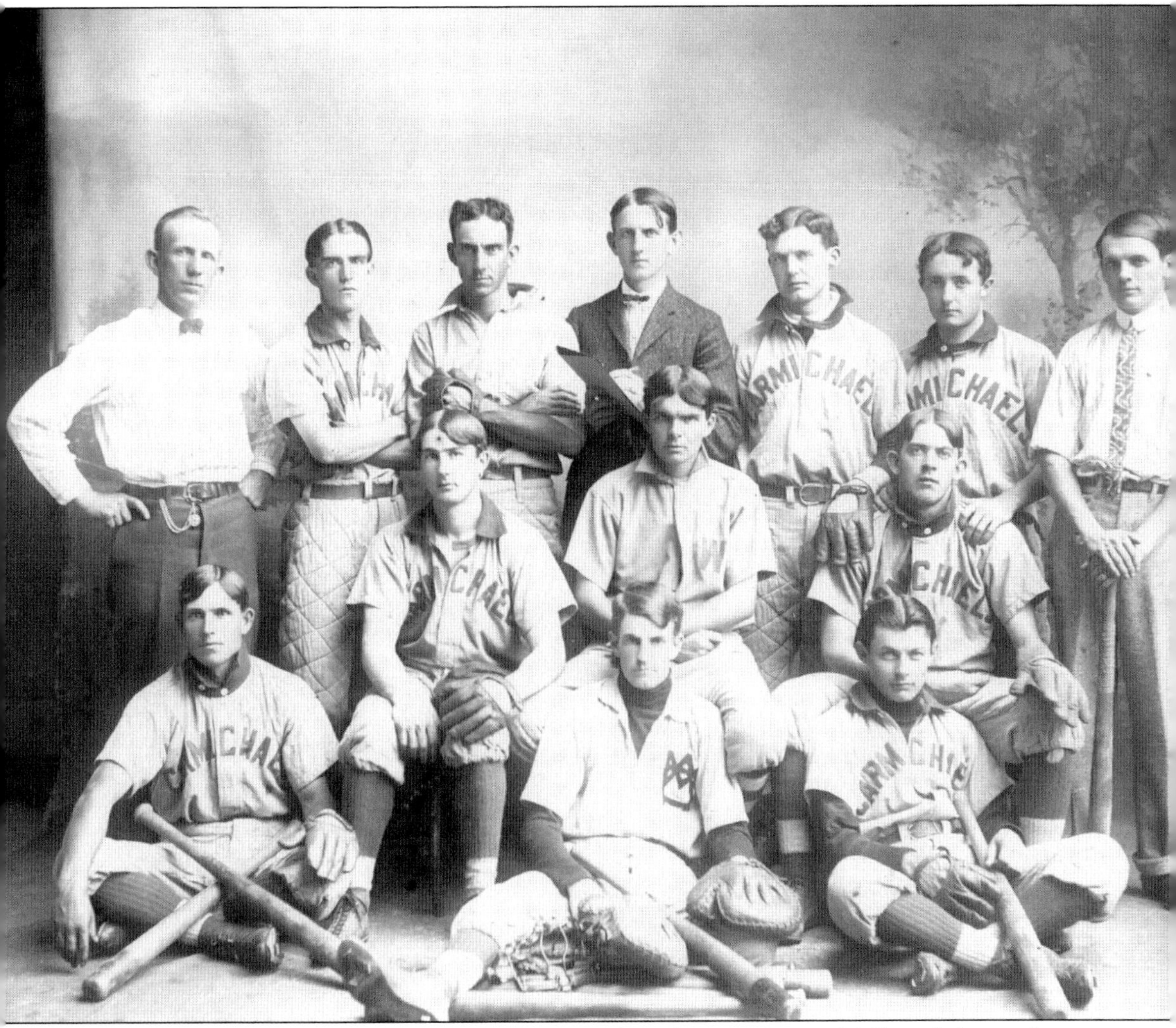

Pictured here are Carmichaels baseball team members from 1903 to 1906. From left to right are (first row) Minor Gladden, Bob Flenniken, and Earl Smith; (second row) Corb Garard, Guy Kerr, and Rickey Hawthorne; (third row) ? Oglin (umpire), Arthur Buchanan, Guy Mundell, Glenn Darrah, Mackie Horner, Frank Barbe, and Earl Miller. Left-handed pitcher Earl Smith pitched for Pittsburgh Catholic College of the Holy Ghost, later known as Duquesne University, and later for a professional baseball team. Guy Kerr, an exceptional catcher, traveled with the St. Louis Bloomer Girls. The Bloomer Girls were one of the first female professional baseball teams but always carried a male catcher. (Courtesy of William Groves.)

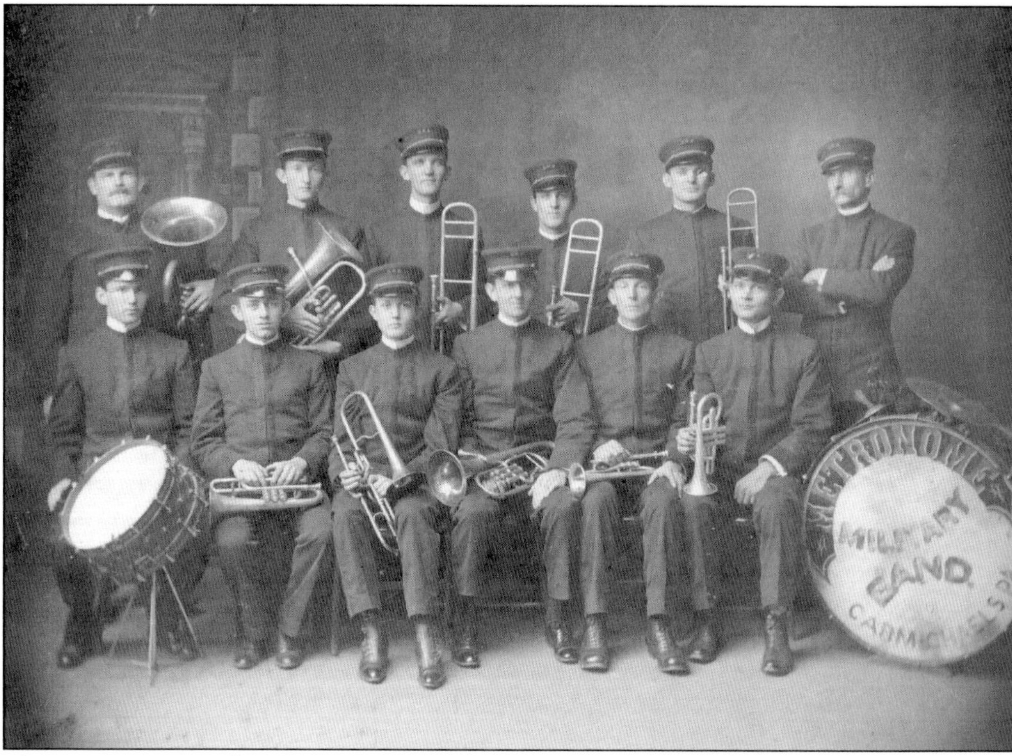

There were numerous bands in Carmichaels and Cumberland Township. The Metronome Military Band was one of them. Pictured are, from left to right, (first row) Sam Guesman, Harry F. Hunnell, Vernon Murdock, Glenn Darrah, Amos Horner, and George Murdock; (second row) Millard F. Hunnell, Barclay F. Davidson, J. Frank Barclay, George H. Burnette, George L. Richey, and Cal Davidson. (Courtesy of William Groves.)

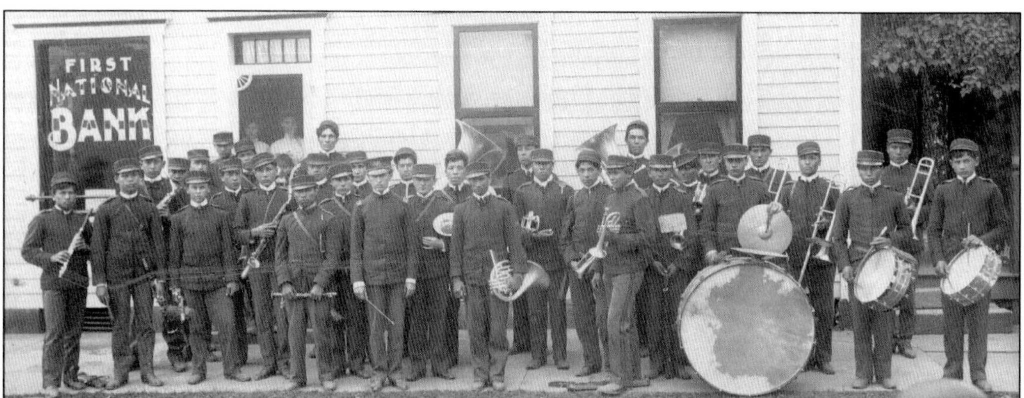

This 1906 photograph shows the Government Indian Band. Under the direction of Lemon H. Wiley, a former student of the Greene Academy and well-known musician, the band played for the Carmichaels Fair that year. The building they are standing in front of was known as the Biddle Building, located on the town square. It housed the First National Bank in 1901. (Courtesy of Greene Academy of Art.)

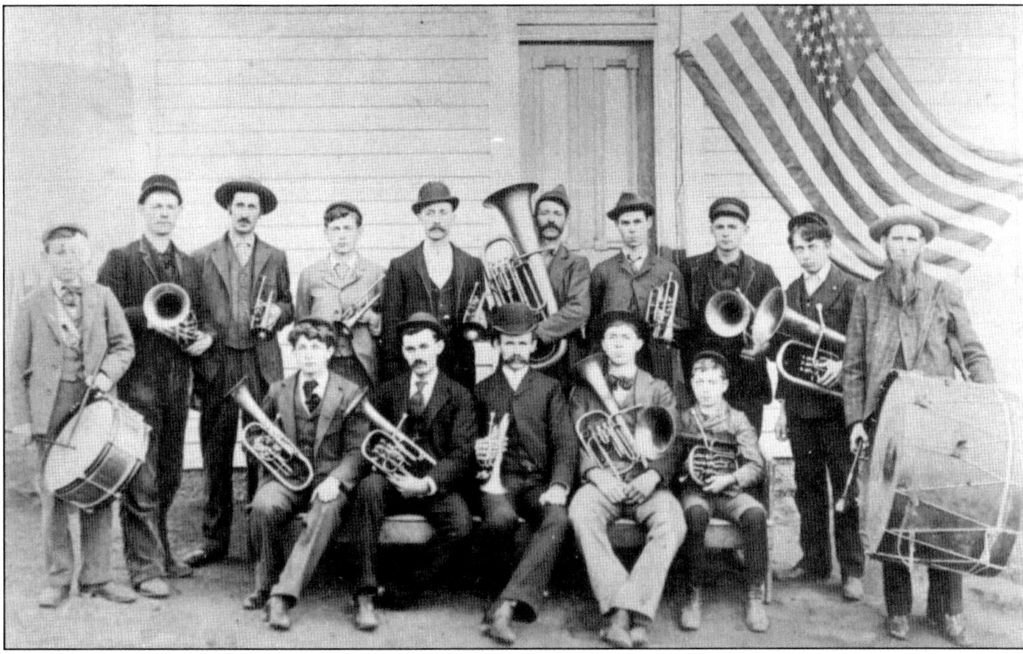

This photograph of the Pierceville "Boo Poopes" was taken prior to 1898. Band members are, from left to right, (first row) Charles Hartley, Joseph Keener, ? Masterzat, Calvin Ullery, and Chester Crumrine; (second row) Jonah Hart, Lewis Ullery, Ellis Parker, Walter Crumrine, Charles Hopton, Amos Rich, Walter Cunningham, Robert Rich, Frank Crumrine, and William Henry Cummins. (Courtesy of William Groves.)

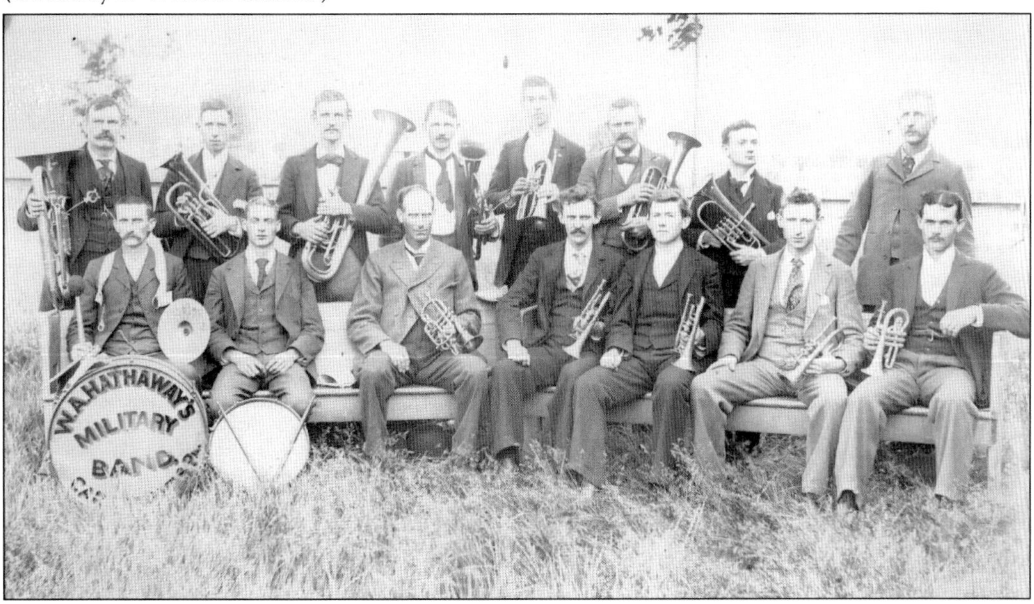

Carmichaels photographer T.W. Rogers took this photograph of the W.A. Hathaway Military Band on Memorial Day, May 30, 1896. Pictured in the first row from left to right are Bob Davidson, Harry Davis, William Smith, Herb Barclay, Ed Wiley, William Pennington, and George Murdock; Among those pictured in the second row are, in unknown order, Millard F. Hunnell, George Pennington, Frank Barclay, Curl Phillips, Ollie Rogers, and William A. Hathaway. (Courtesy William Groves.)

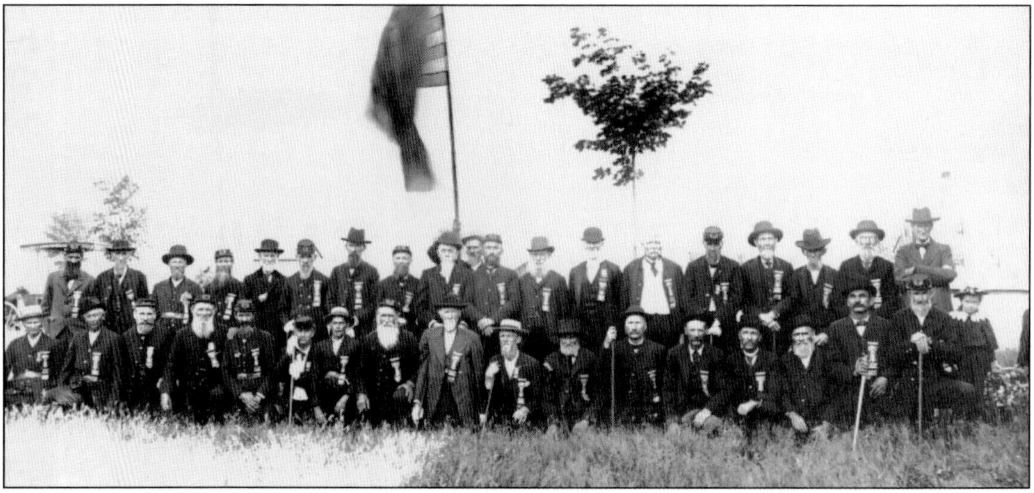

Seen here on Memorial Day, May 30, 1896, are members of the Grand Army of the Republic, former soldiers who served on the Union side during the Civil War. From left to right are (first row) George Eicher, unidentified, Frank Clark, George Crow, unidentified, Samuel Roberts, Brice Evans, James Reese Cummins, unidentified, Canada Davis, William Harvey "Blind Billy" Crago, unidentified, Henry Huston, three unidentified, Jim Birch, Thomas Crago, Mary Stone (child), and Elvis Stone (child); (second row) Truman Kelley, unidentified, Abe Guesman, unidentified, Dr. John Laidley, Alec Alfree, Pete Syphers, George Daugherty, Dr. Howard, Frank Fisher (holding flag), Sesley Bayard, unidentified, Billy Martin, Russell Armstrong, Huston Kerr, Major Josiah Harvey Rea, Mr. Ewart, Captain Hiram H. Cree, and George Stone. At one time, the organization owned the Greene Academy in Carmichaels, where they met until the last member passed away. (Courtesy of Greene Academy of Art.)

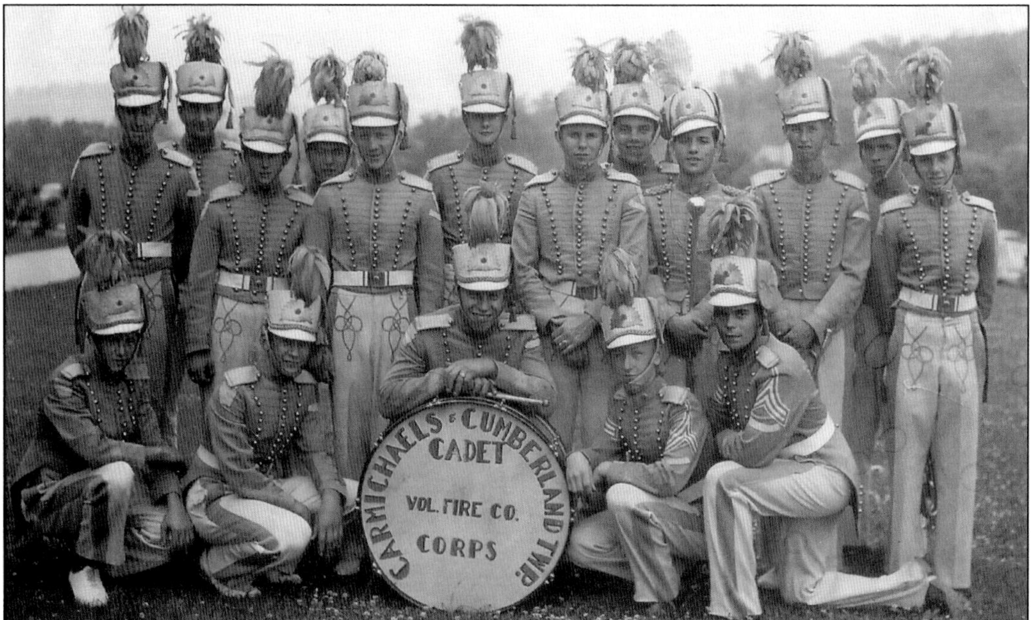

Pictured is the Carmichaels & Cumberland Township Cadet Volunteer Fire Company Corp. Two members of the band have been identified. James Baily is kneeling on the far right, and standing fourth from left is George "Duck Foot" McCombs. (Courtesy of Carmichaels mayor David Jack.)

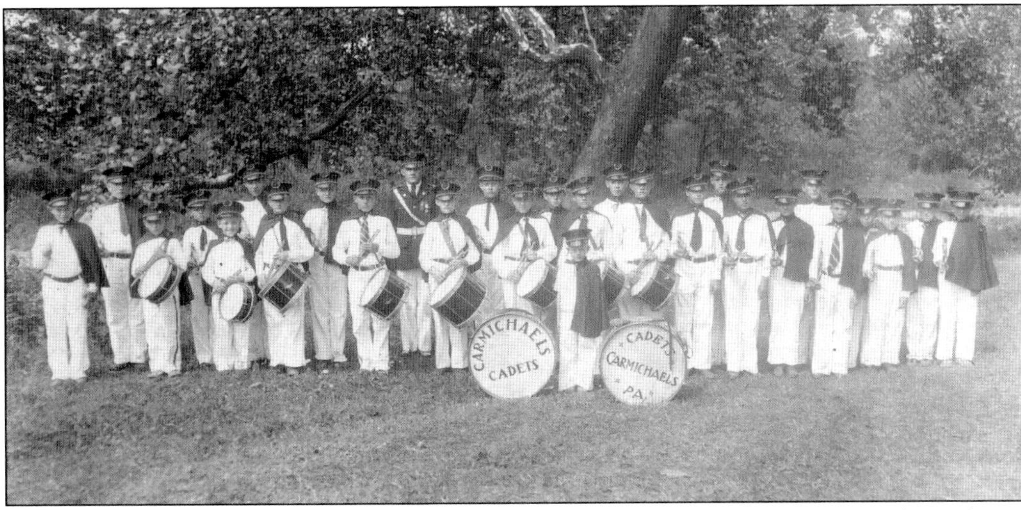

The Carmichaels Boy Cadet Drum and Bugle Corps played in every major parade in the tri-county area for five years. On May 30, 1932, they celebrated their fifth anniversary. The Corps had 27 members, the youngest being five-year-old junior drum major Woodie Hathaway. Other members were Inghram Hewitt, William Deems, Glenn and Harold Donley, Zigmond and Walter Jankowski, George McCombs, Hugh and James Baily, Glenn Allison, Harvey McMinn, Ralph Bari, Earl Burnette, Edward Urbany, Paul Toth, Wilbur Barclay, Robert Solly, Clarence Baker, Douglas Maple, Melio Bertugli, Lloyd Smith, Victor Moranza, Raymond Jordan, Francis Grimm, George Toth, Jack Hathaway, and William Hathaway. (Courtesy of Carmichaels mayor David Jack.)

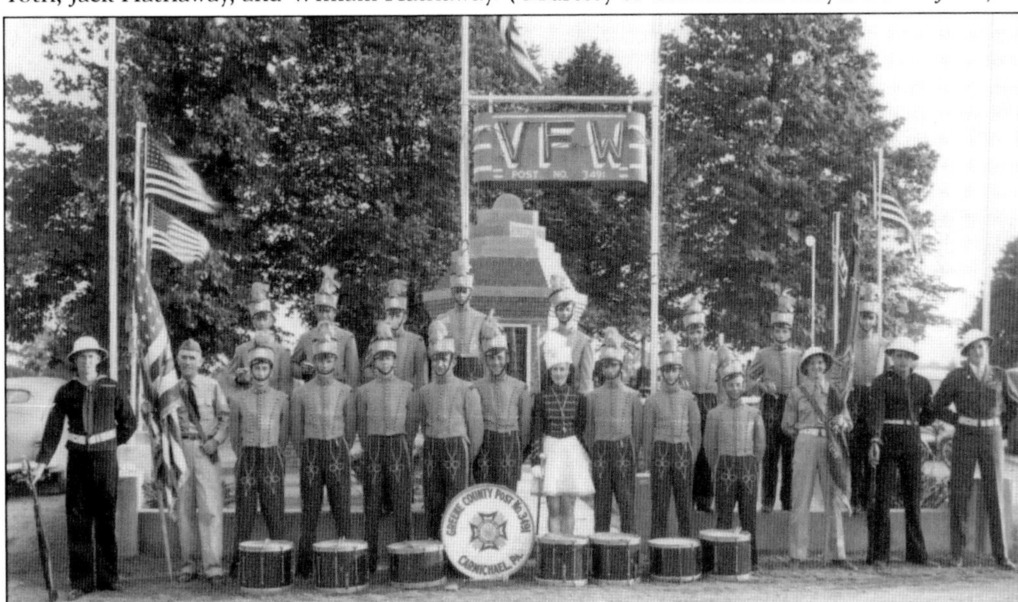

Pictured is the Carmichaels Veterans of Foreign Wars (VFW) Post No. 3491 band. They are standing in the triangle between Old Waynesburg and Ceylon Roads. Behind the band is the honor roll that was erected by the Ladies Auxiliary during World War II. Listed on the honor roll were the names of those from the area who were serving in the military. In 1976, when the nearby VFW building was sold, the honor roll was demolished; soon after, the building was destroyed by fire. (Courtesy of Walter "Blackie" Markoweich.)

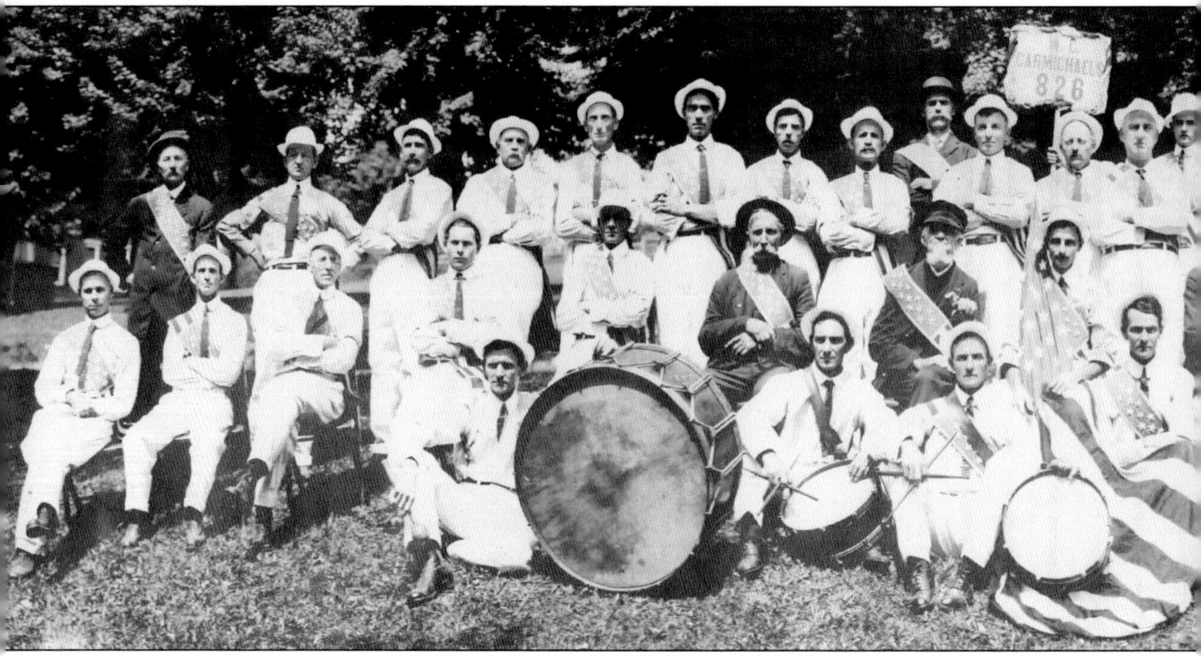

Pictured are unidentified members of Washington Camp No. 826 of the Patriotic Order of the Sons of America (POS of A) of Carmichaels. The group was instituted on December 22, 1911, and went defunct during the 1939–1940 term. All POS of A camps were named "Washington Camp" in honor of Pres. George Washington and were assigned a number. The original charter members for the Carmichaels camp were Charles L. Riley, Lynn G. Barnhart, J.A. Grooms, R.I. Stewart, Paul R. Hathaway, Dan Crago, W.F. Wychoff, John Burnet, George F. McMinn,

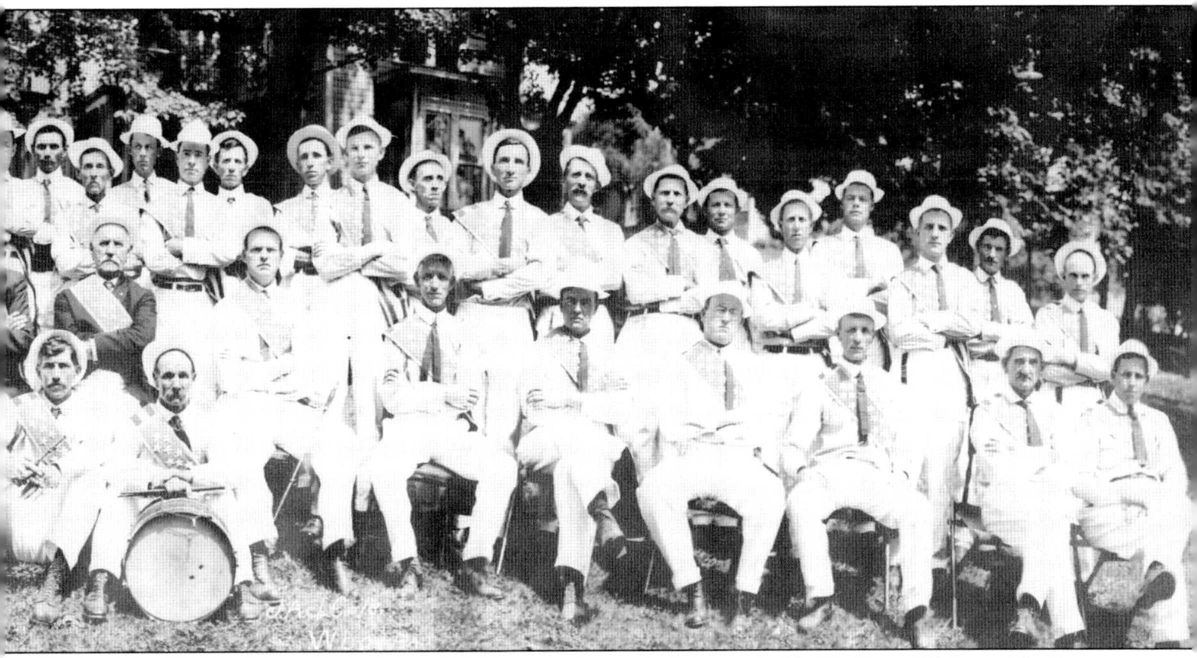

Thomas J. Hathaway, Fremont F. Solomon, Perry A. Myers, C.H. Phillips, William H. Crago, E.B. Schmitz, Neri Hart, Robert Kerr, Jesse Dunston, W.L. Dunston, Edgar Grooms, Russell Crago, Briton W. Crago, R. Ramsey, F.C. Haines, John G. Areford, J.C. Burnett, John Barclay, J.W. McCombs, H.T. Durr, Carl Williamson, R.G. Ramsey, Albert Guesman, H.E. Griffith, John H. Mafrel, J.F. Flenniken, James Birch, R.H. Crago, C.A. McWilliams, and J.C. Long. (Courtesy of Greene Academy of Art.)

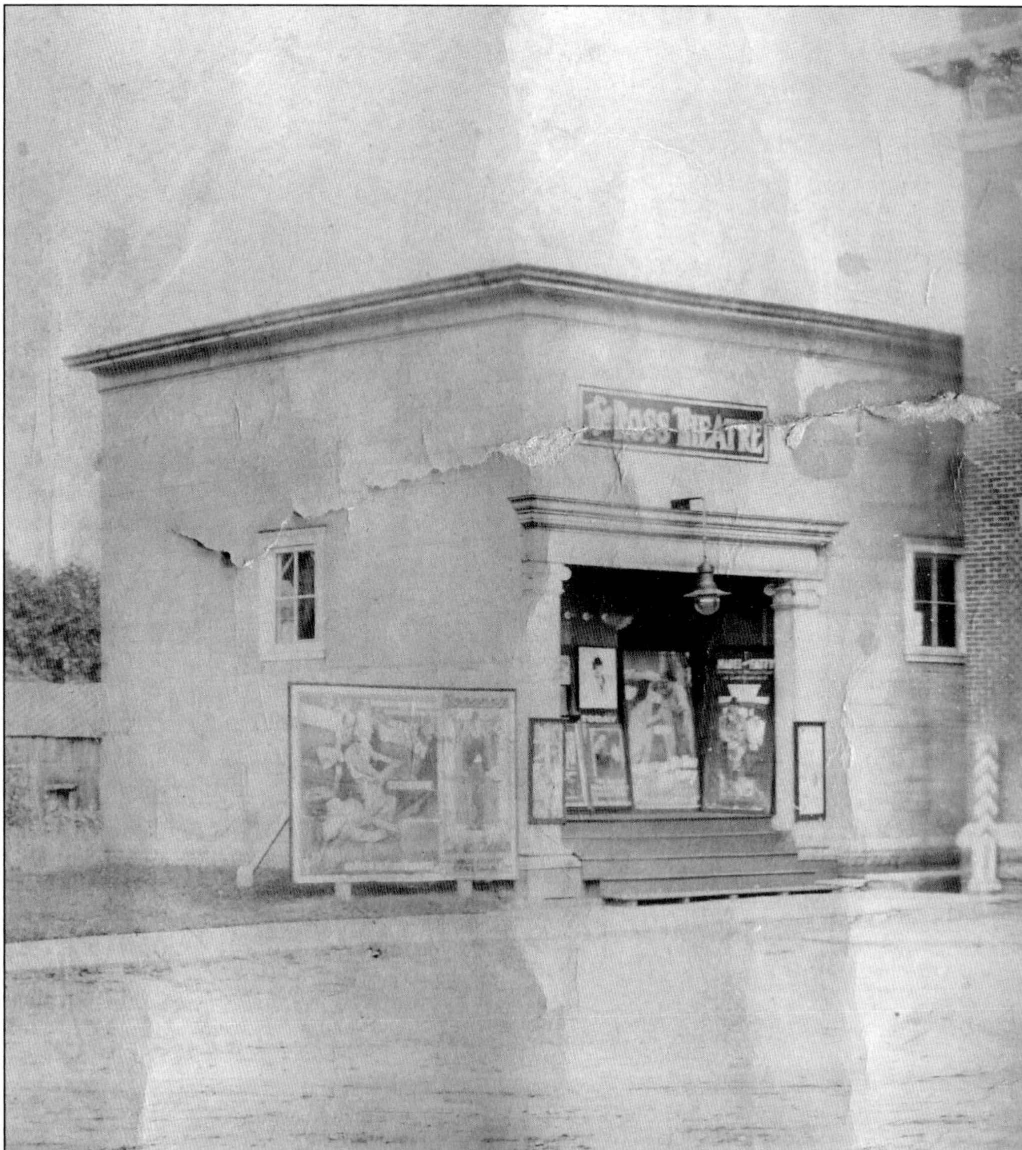

The Ross Theatre in Carmichaels opened on the public square in 1913. Music was played on a player piano for the silent movies. All children under the age of 16 sat in the front rows, with boys on one side and girls on the other. The first talking movie at the theater was *Happy Days* in 1930. The building was later purchased by John Lund. Lund added an addition to the building, and it became known as the Lund Theater. In 1946, a new Lund Theater was opened next to the previous one and was in operation until 1968. The last movie shown was *In Cold Blood*. According to an article in the February 14, 1940, *Morning Herald*, a second movie theater was scheduled to open in the community of Fairdale, a quarter mile away from Carmichaels, in June of that year; however, it never opened. (Courtesy of Greene County Historical Society and Museum.)

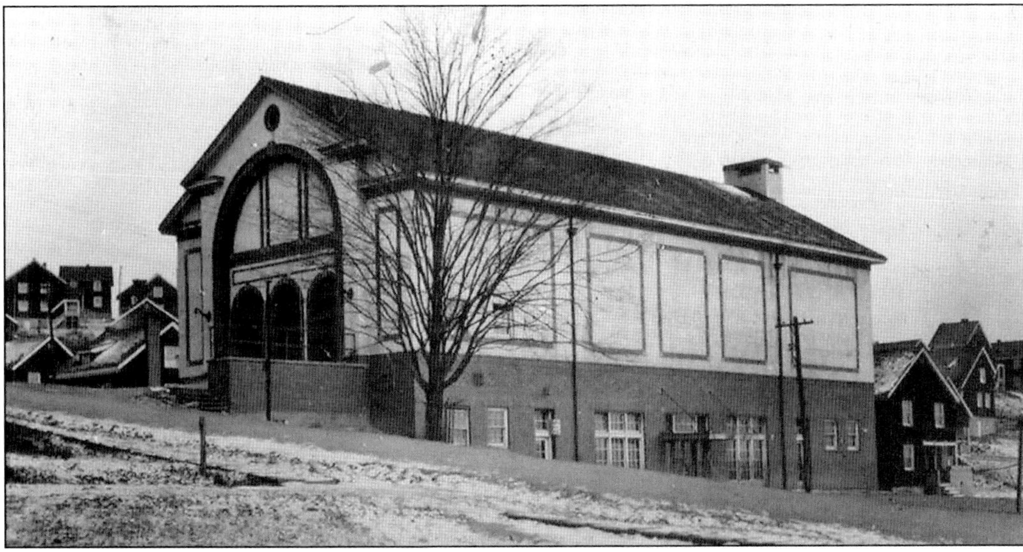

Construction of the Nemacolin Amusement Building began on July 9, 1920. It contained a 550-person theater, bowling alleys, pool tables, a restaurant, and barbershop. The opening performance of the theater was on March 3, 1921. (Courtesy of Brice and Linda Rush and the Robert Korcheck collection.)

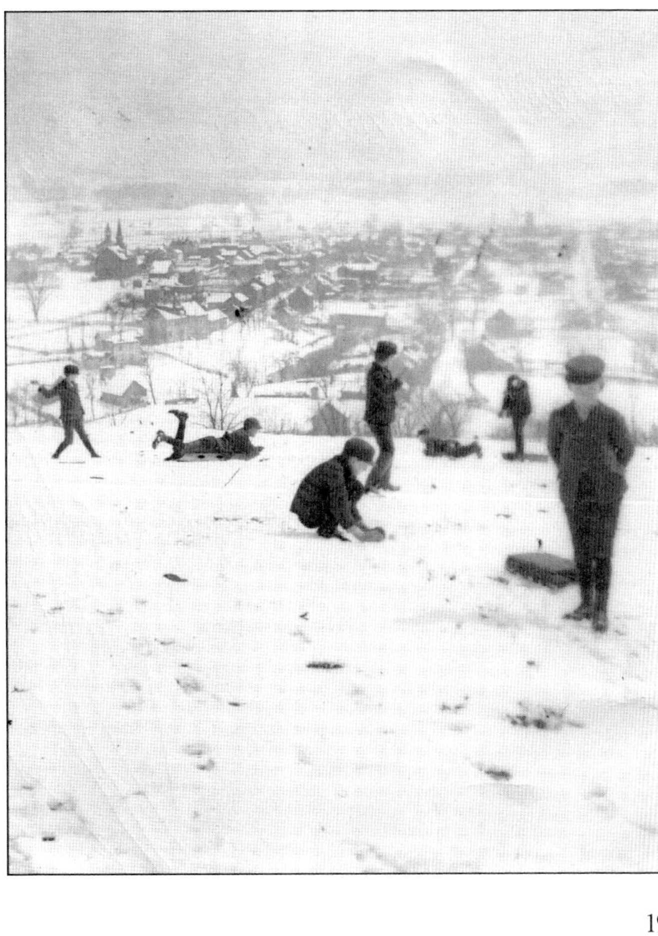

This photograph shows a group of unidentified children having fun throwing snowballs and sledding on what is known as Town Hill, located above Old Town. Based on the buildings in the background, the photograph was likely taken between 1895 and 1901. (Courtesy of Greene County Historical Society and Museum.)

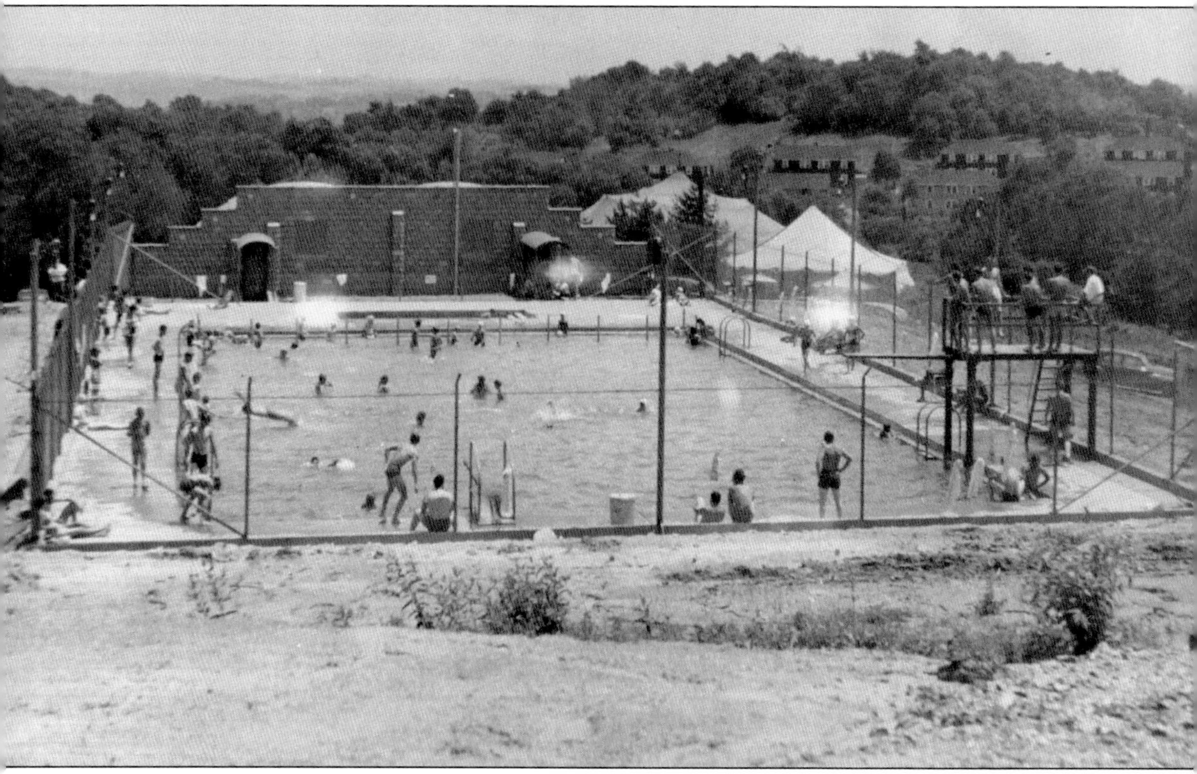

A favorite spot to cool off on summer days and to spend time with friends was the Nemacolin Swimming Pool, which opened May 30, 1950. The last season the pool was in operation was the summer of 1977. (Courtesy of Flenniken Memorial Library.)

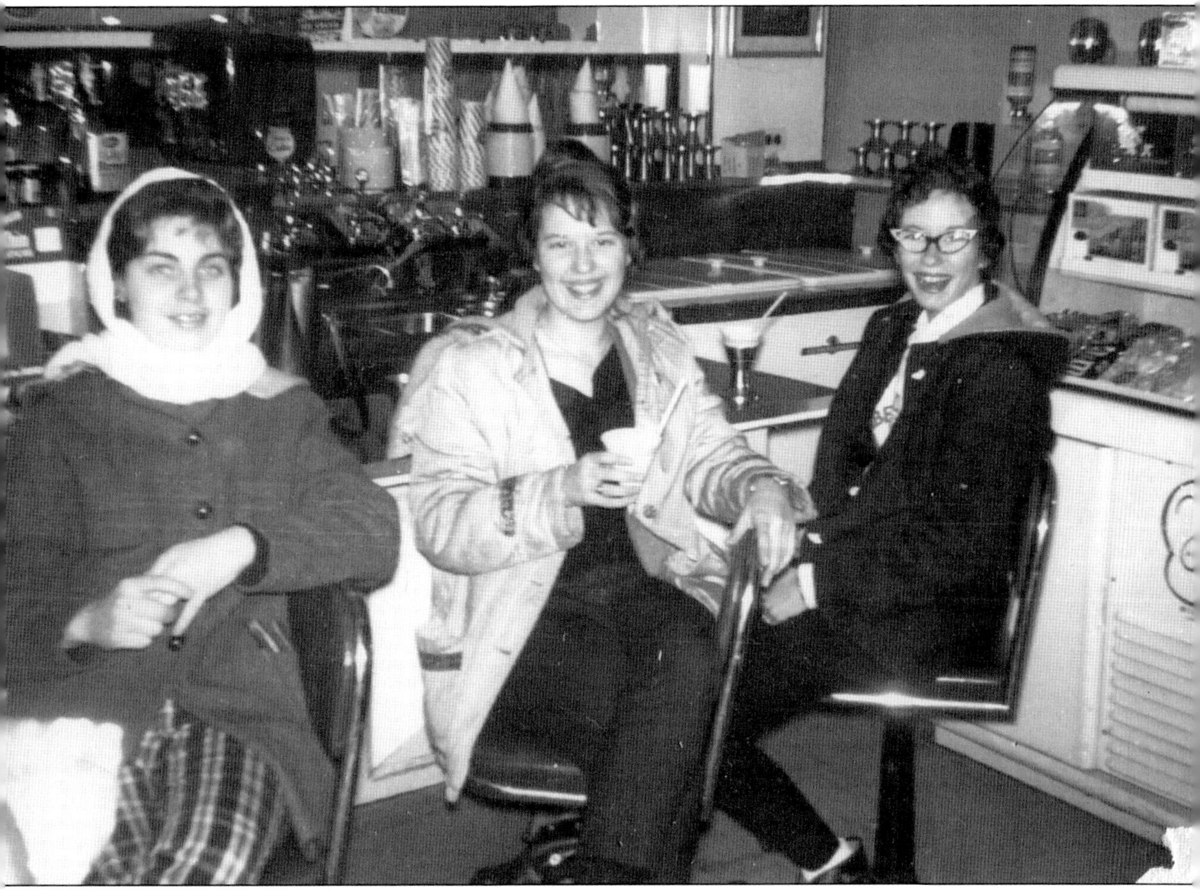

A favorite place for teens to gather was Taylor's Drugstore, owned by Bill and Irene Taylor. The drugstore, located on the town square, was known for its soda fountain. Everyone who was raised in Carmichaels recalls the great milkshakes, ice cream sodas, and root beer floats made by Mabel McMinn. These young ladies are all smiles enjoying their beverages. From left to right are Clara King, Mary Catherine Burnette, and Kathie Clark. (Courtesy of Mary Catherine Burnette Kirk.)

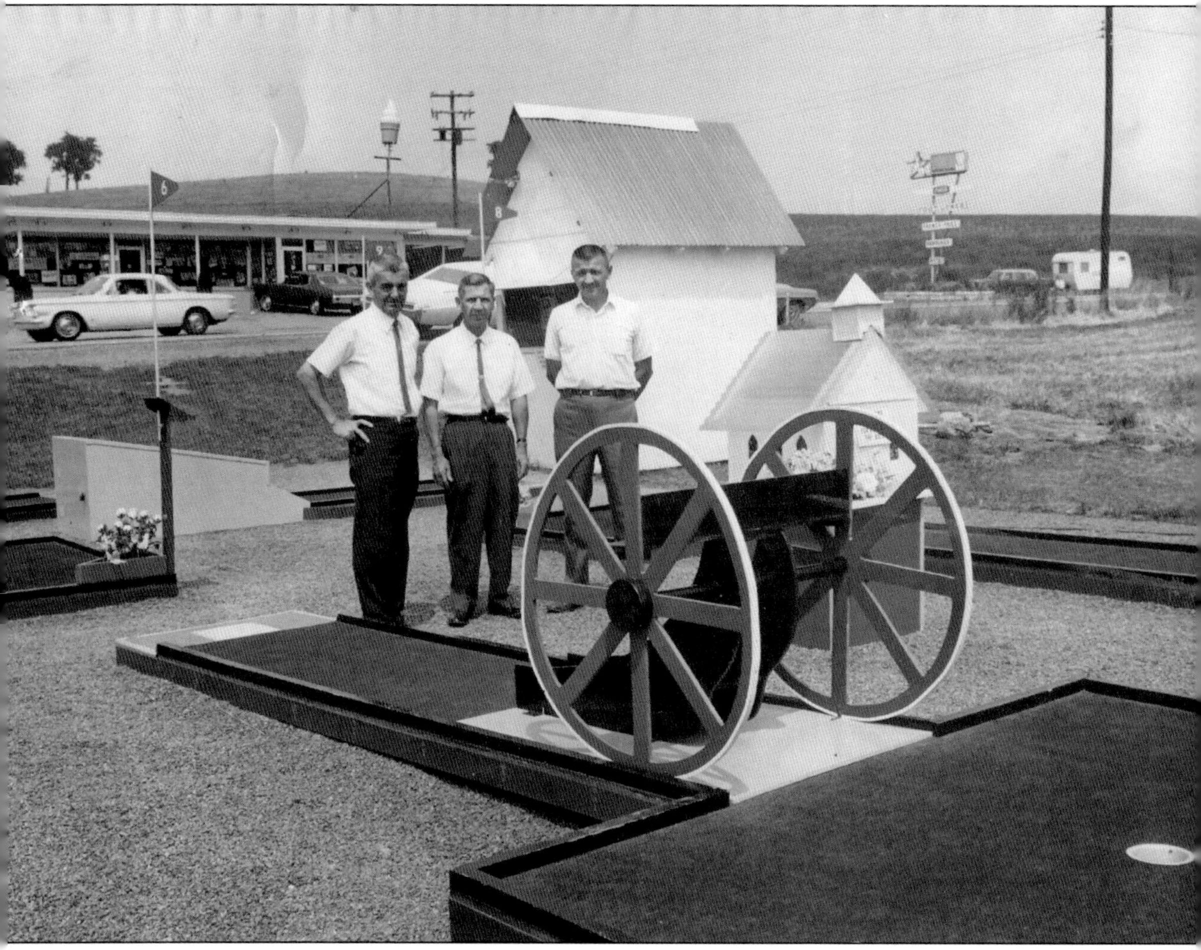

Another popular place to relax, eat, enjoy ice cream, and have some fun was Hoge's Dairy Bar and miniature golf course, owned by John Hoge. The dairy bar in the background was a popular place to cool off on a hot summer day. Pictured at the golf course are, from left to right, James Yeash, Albert Yelenik, and Henry Bacon. (Courtesy of Flenniken Memorial Library.)

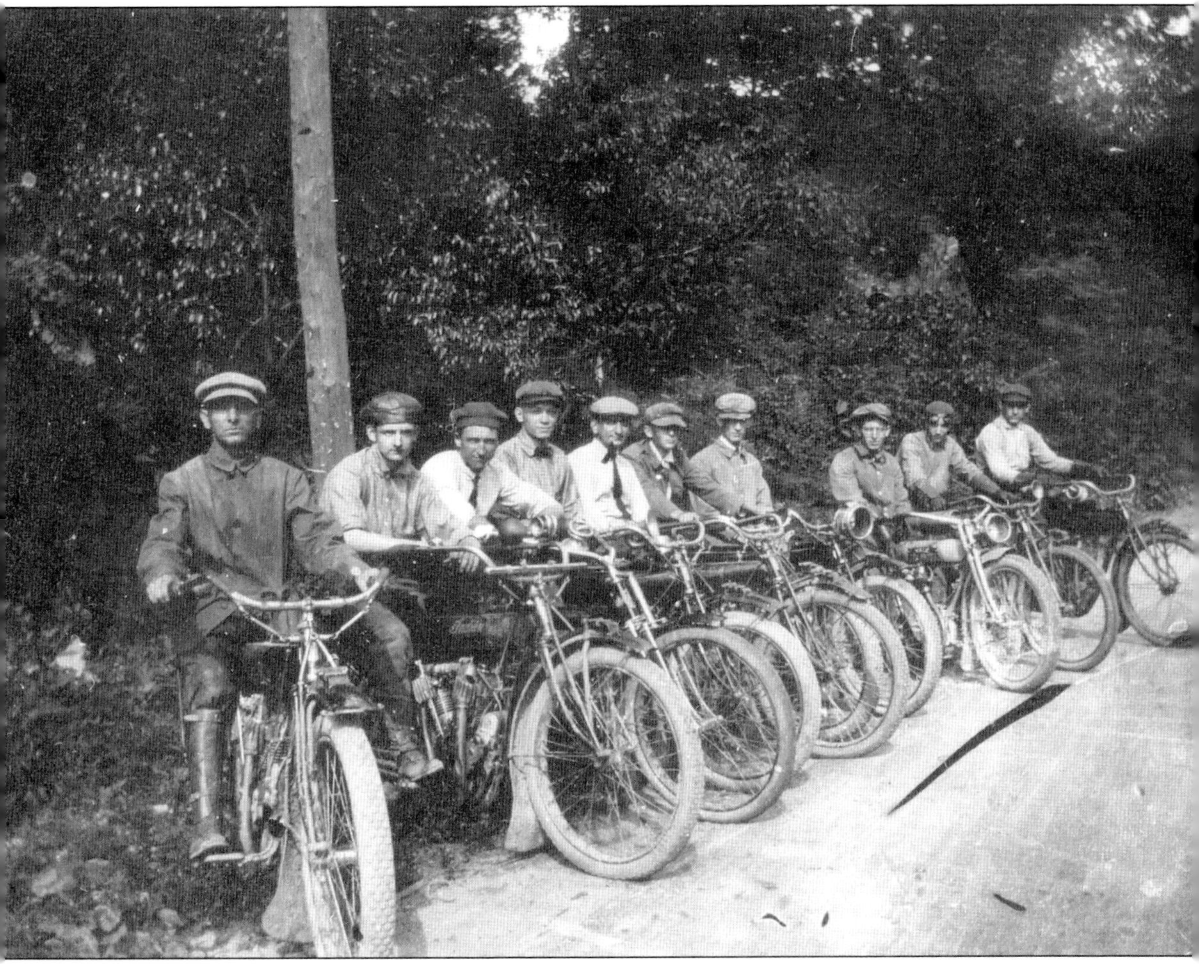

Pictured here is a group of men from Cumberland Township, led by John Talmage Hart, on their Indian motorcycles, six of whom toured the United States. (Courtesy of Greene County Historical Society and Museum.)

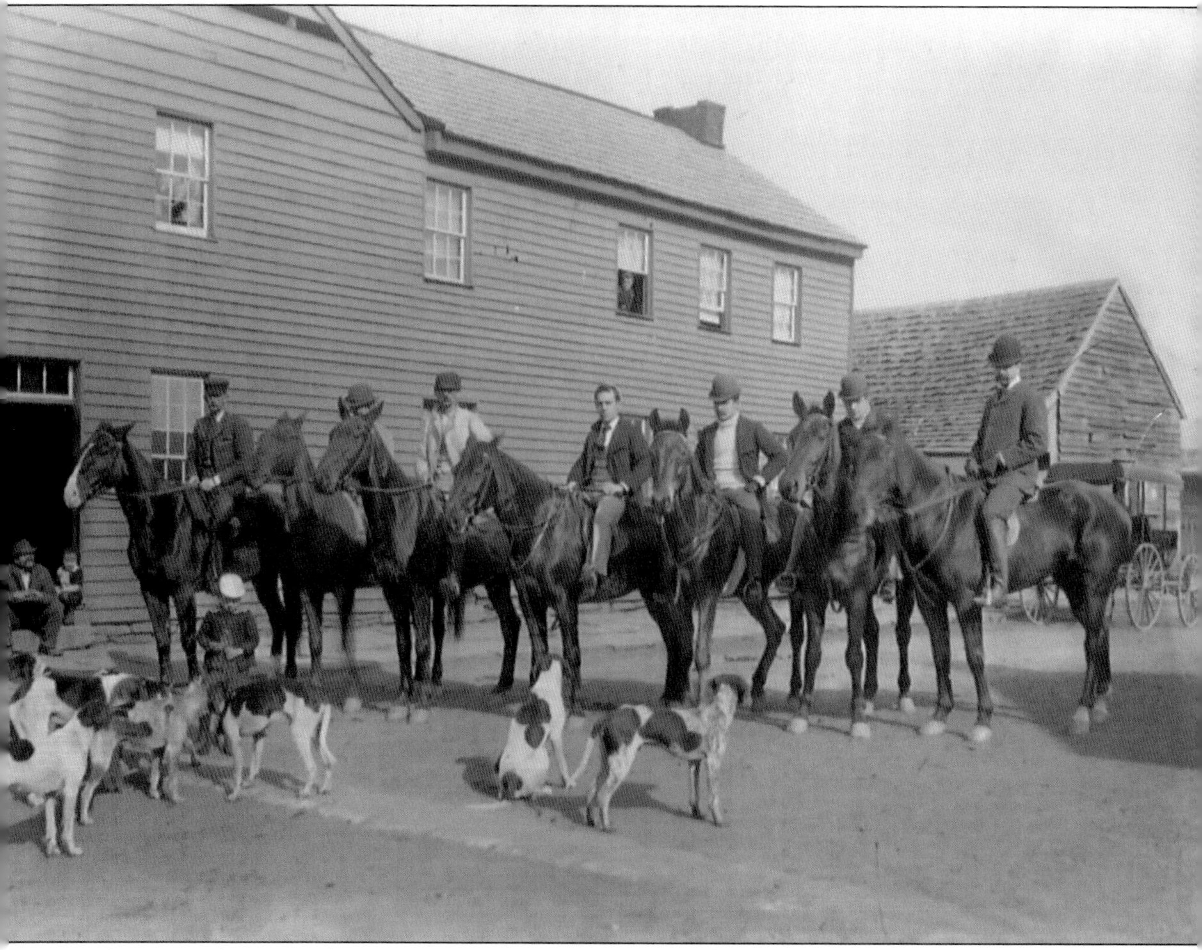

This November 1893 photograph shows a gathering of men, horses, and their dogs in Carmichaels; they are preparing for an upcoming foxhunt. J. Fremont Flenniken and Gus Moredock are in the photograph; however, their locations are unknown. The two-story, wood-frame building in the background is the Red Onion Tavern, owned by James D. Flenniken. The tavern had a large covered front porch, which faced Market Street and the town square. (Courtesy of Greene Academy of Art.)

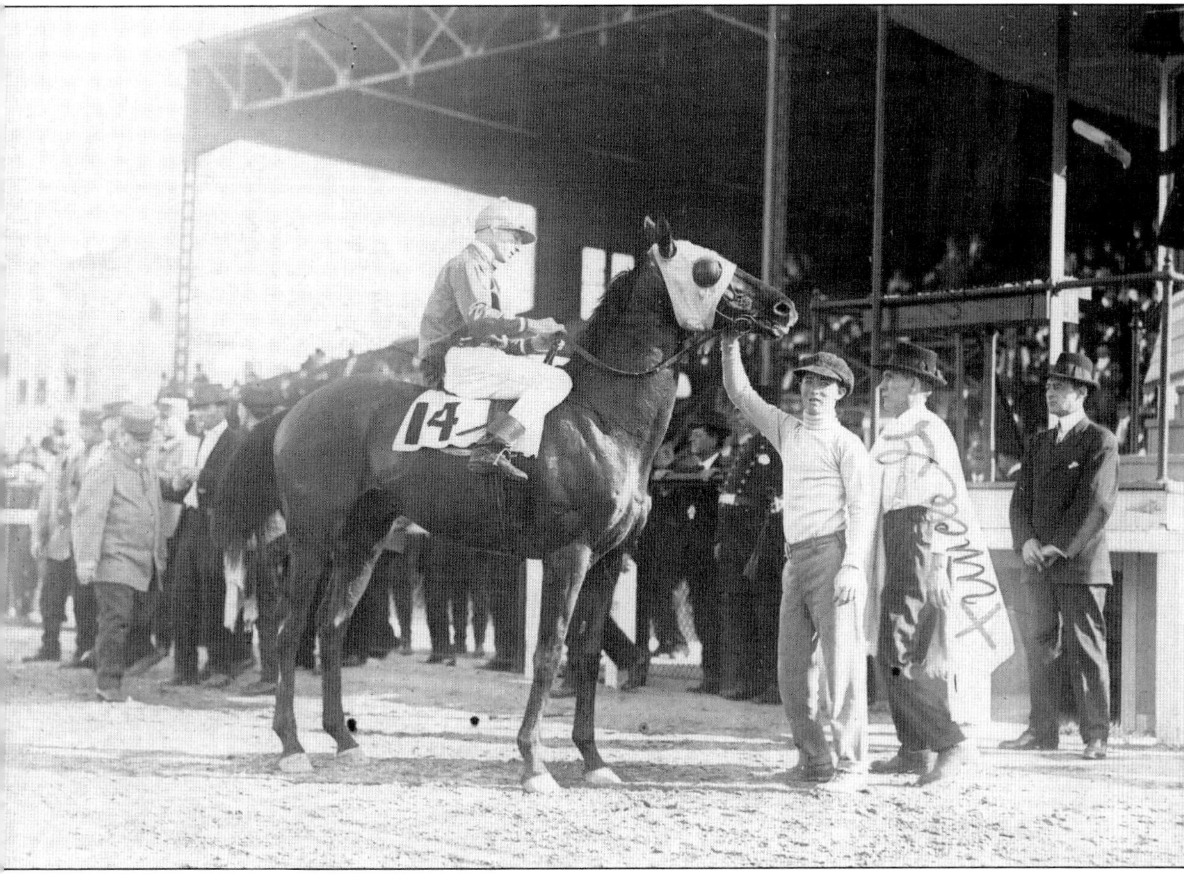

From 1852 to 1935, the Carmichaels Fair attracted thousands of spectators and participants. At one time, it was known as the Greene County Fair. The first fairgrounds were located off of East George Street, Hudson Street, and Liberty Avenue, the location of the present-day housing development Cumberland Village. Seen here is George Kerr (standing second from right) with his horse Royal Tea. (Courtesy of Carole Gideon.)

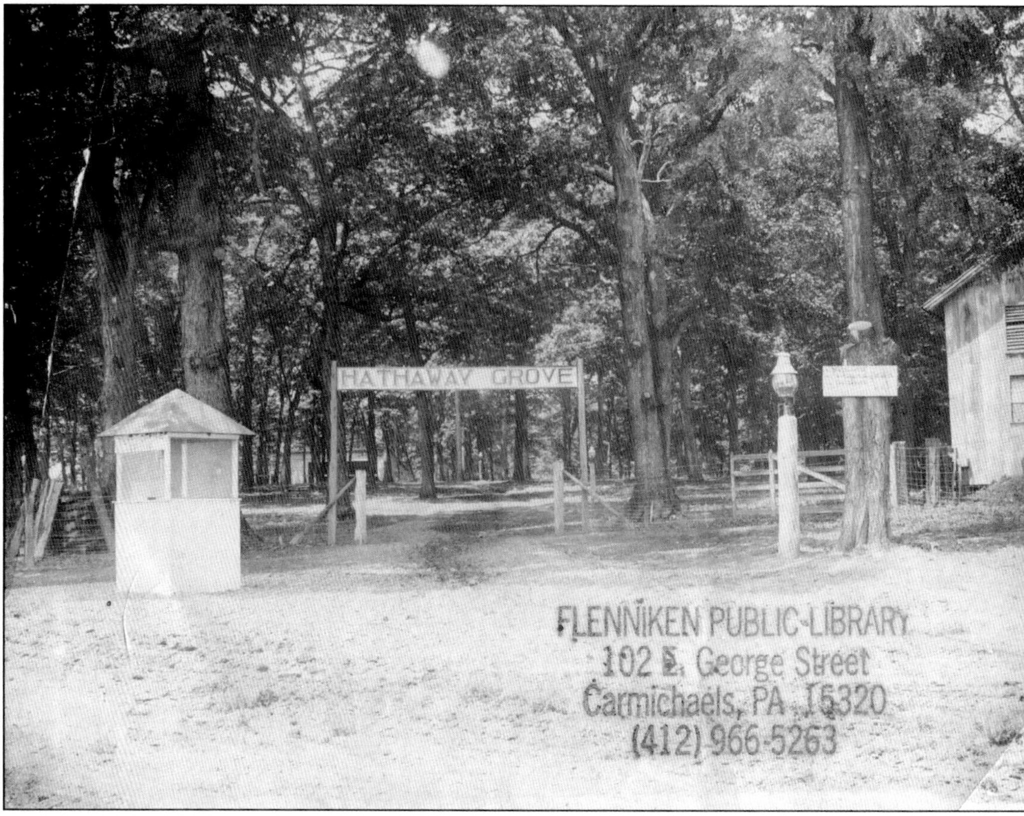

Hathaway Grove was founded by William Anderson Hathaway. In July 1935, the chamber of commerce erected a rustic log cabin for the caretaker to reside in. The property was later sold and became known as Joyland Park. (Courtesy of Flenniken Memorial Library.)

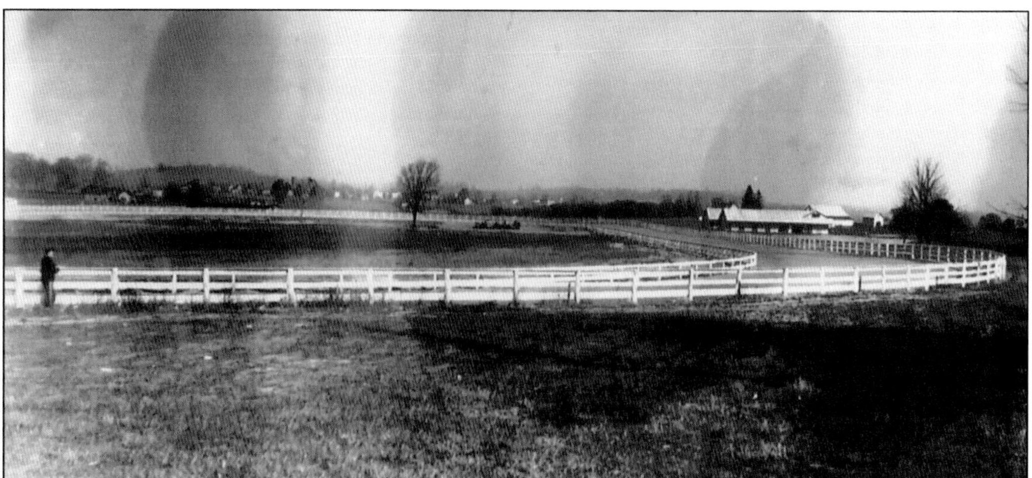

This photograph shows the fairgrounds located between Route 88 and Ceylon Road, the current location of Wana B. Park. This was the second location of the Carmichaels Fair. (Courtesy of Flenniken Memorial Library from the Hester Rutter collection.)

Two

People, Places, and Things

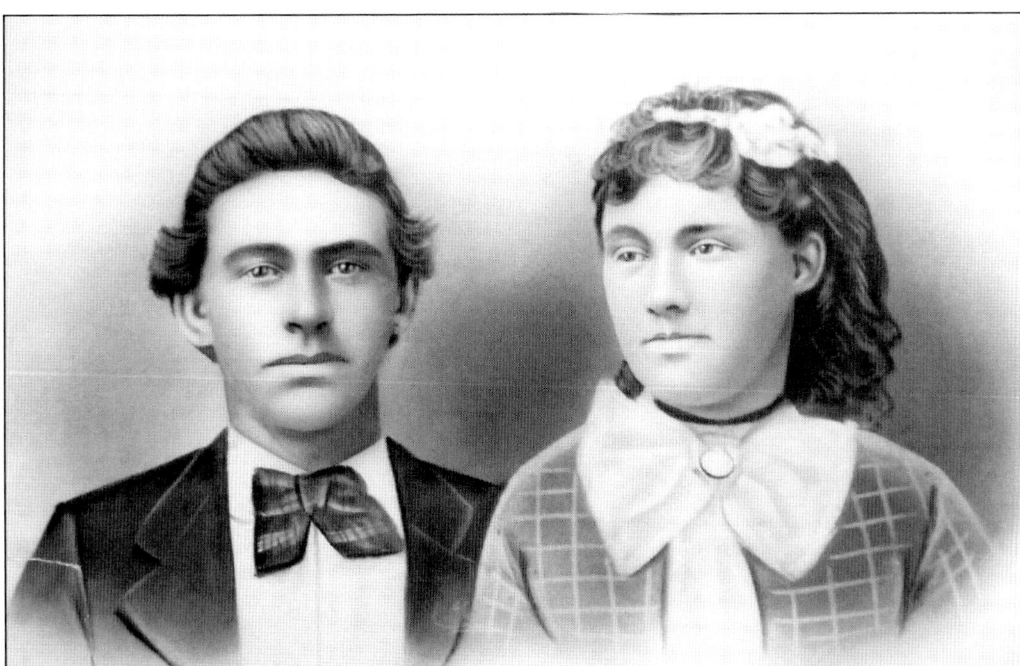

This portrait of William F. and Mary A. Flenniken hangs in the Flenniken Memorial Library, named in their memory by their son Earl T. Flenniken. (Courtesy of Flenniken Memorial Library.)

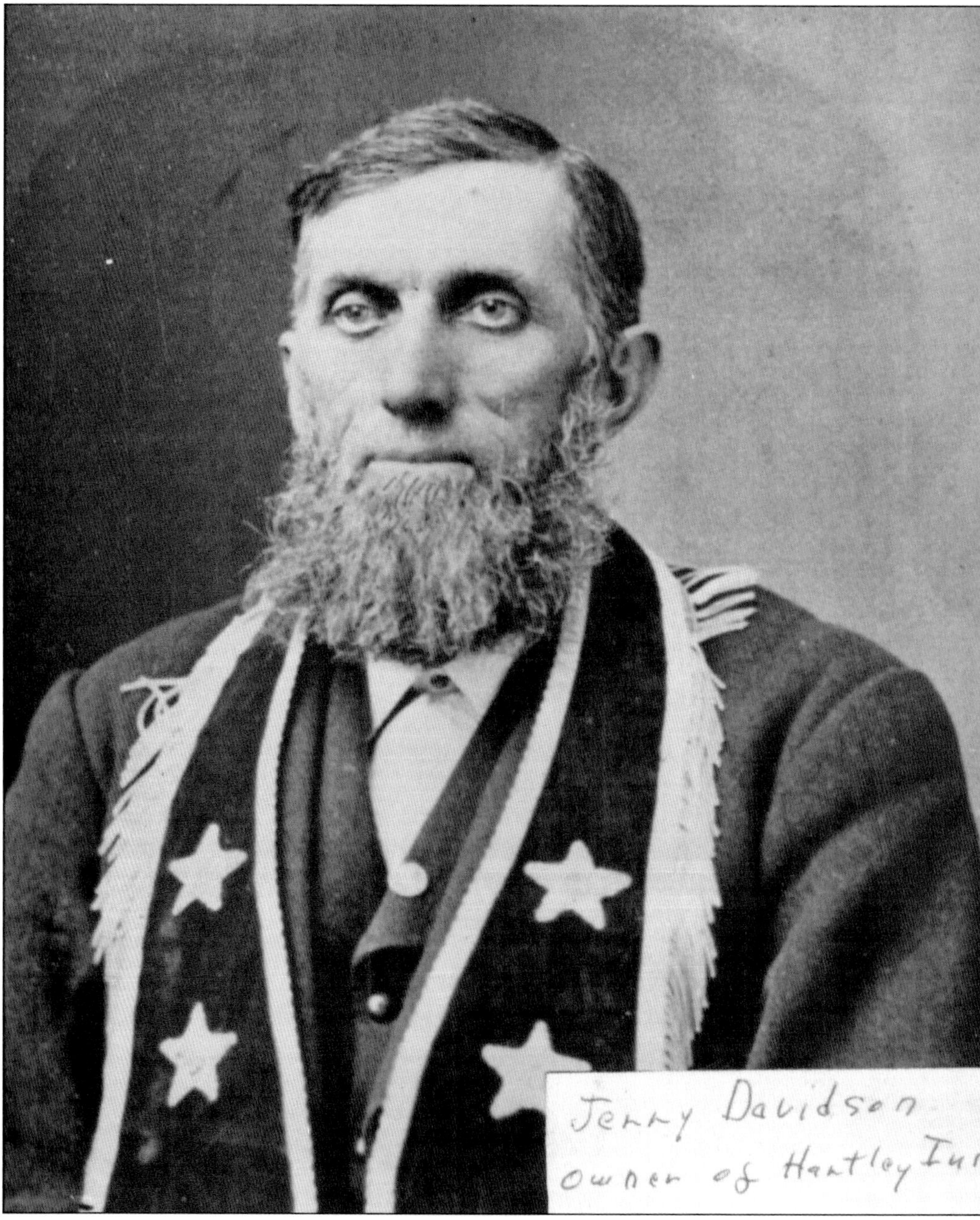

This is Jeremiah Davidson, owner of the former Davidson House, which is now known as the Hartley Inn, located on the town square. (Courtesy of the Greene Academy of Art.)

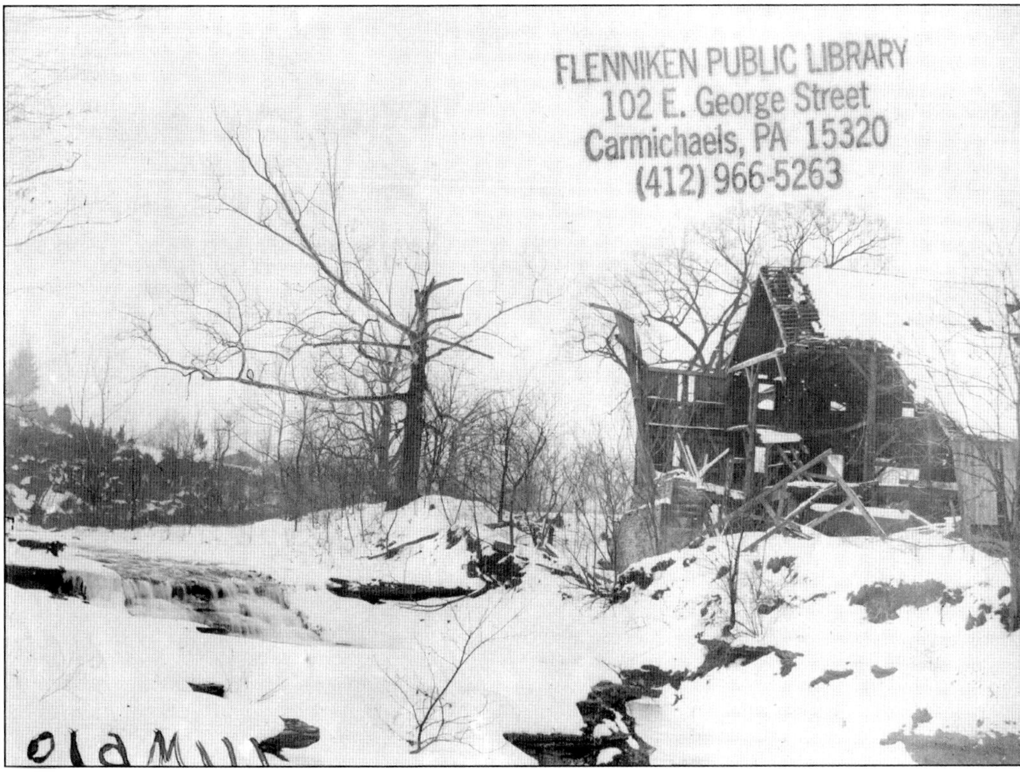

This photograph shows the remains of the Curl Mill on the banks of Muddy Creek. The mill was owned and operated by John Curl. On October 4, 1871, Curl was turning the flywheel of his sawmill engine, which caught his arm and threw him under the flywheel and drum. The flywheel was cutting him on one side and the drum on the other. He had to lie there until someone finally came to see why the steam was coming out of the mill and stop the engine to remove him. His injuries were so severe that his right arm had to be amputated. (Courtesy of Flenniken Memorial Library.)

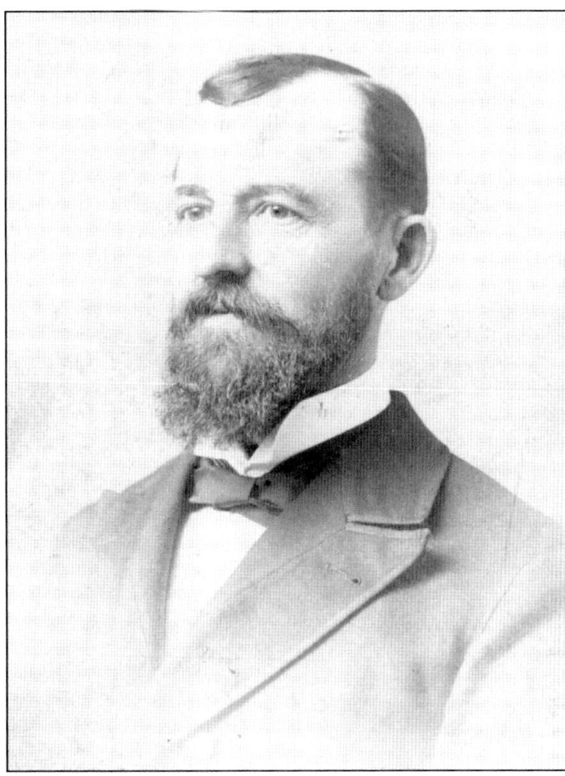

Pictured here is Dr. Andrew J. Gibbons. It is reported that Dr. Gibbons owned the first automobile in Carmichaels, which he kept in the stable behind his three-story home and medical office on East George Street. (Courtesy of Greene County Historical Society and Museum.)

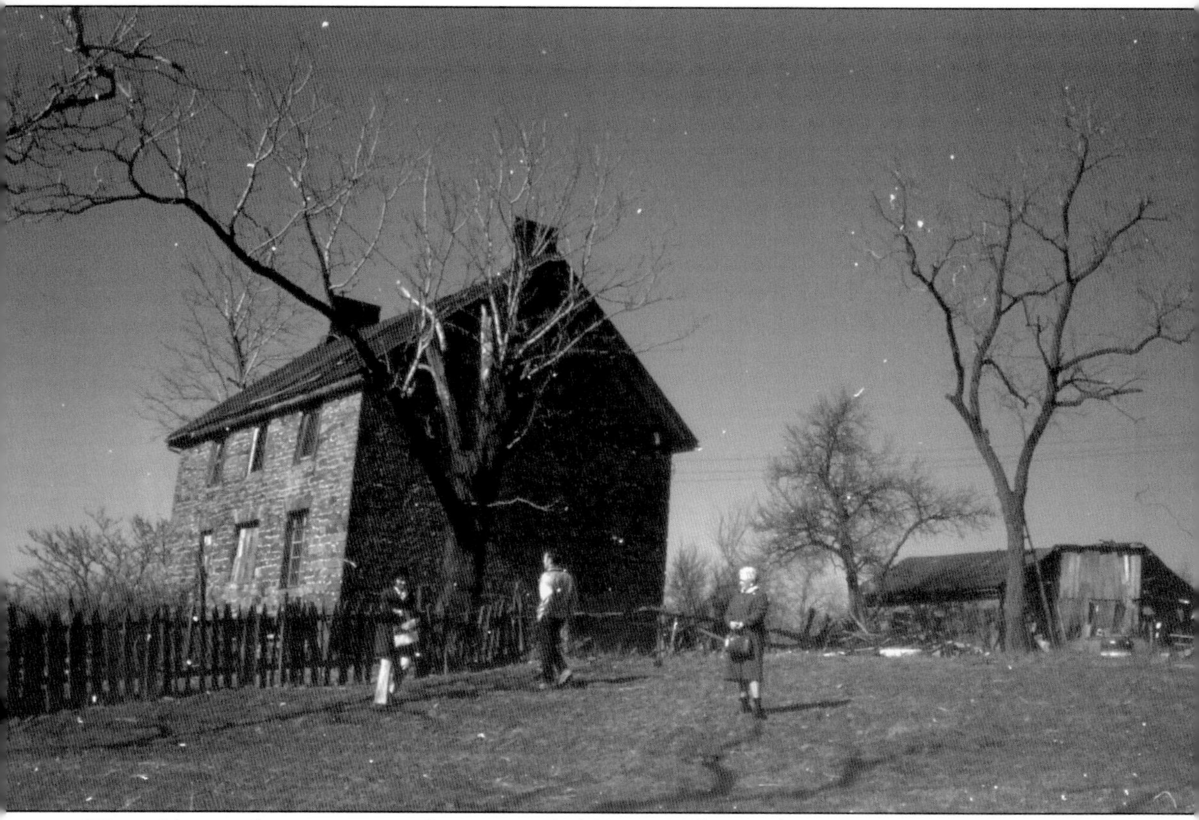

This old stone house was on what was called Town Hill, now known as Hill Road. This hill overlooks Old Town and Carmichaels. Records indicate the house was built in the late 1760s and was a stopping place for stagecoaches. It was known as the John Adamson farm. There were four rooms on the first floor and four on the second floor, each having its own fireplace. Separate buildings on the property were used as a washhouse and kitchen. It has always been rumored that, during his time as a surveyor, George Washington spent a night in this tavern. Anyone who grew up in Old Town will share fond memories of visiting this stone house when John and Agnes Sekora, along with their children and grandchildren, lived there. Although the shell of the house is still standing, the interior was destroyed by fire many years ago. (Courtesy of Flenniken Memorial Library.)

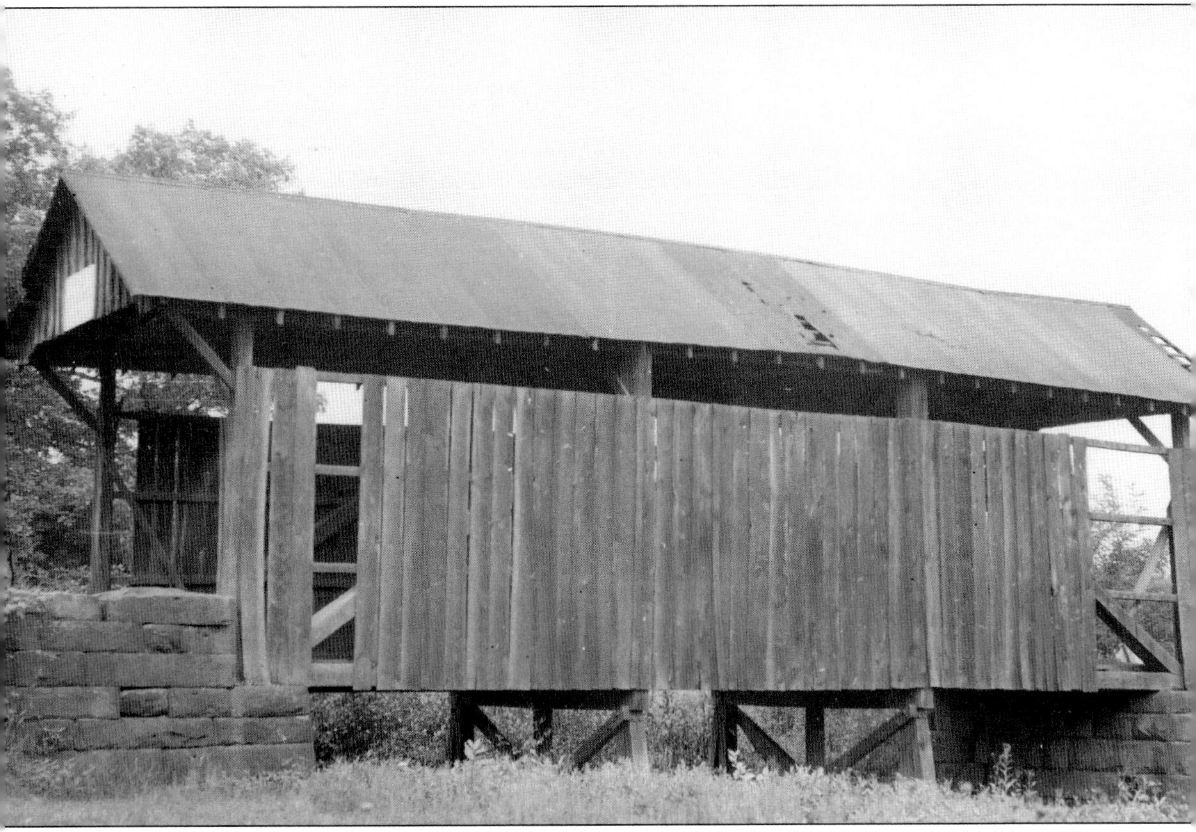

No longer standing, this covered bridge, built in 1880, once stood at the west end of the village of Paisley over Whiteley Creek, which separated Cumberland Township from Monongahela Township. This bridge was not far from where the McCann ferry was located and the area where one of the most notorious murders was committed—the murder of William McCausland in 1888—for which two men were found guilty and hanged. (Courtesy of Greene County Historical Society and Museum.)

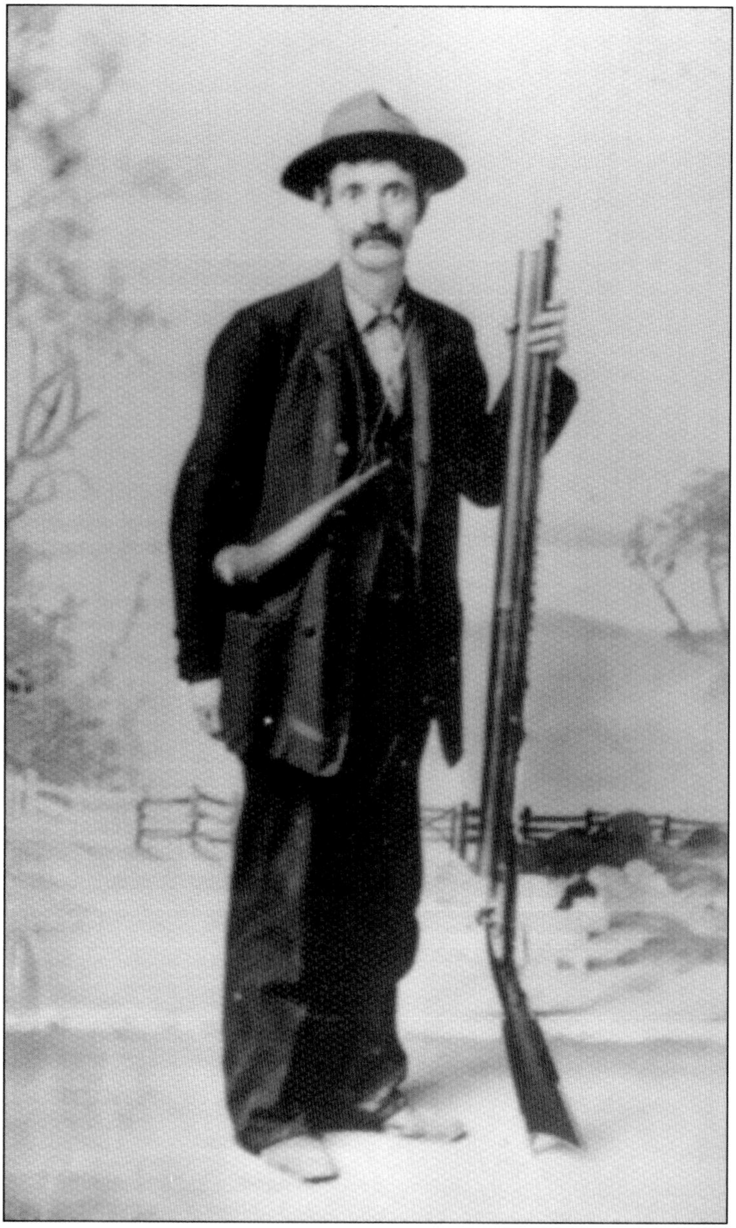

Pictured here is John Reuben McMinn, son of Luther and Caroline (Crago) McMinn and grandson of John and Eleanor (Flenniken) Crago. John McMinn was an exceptional sharpshooter and liked to participate in shooting matches. At one of the matches, five shots were to be fired from 75 yards at a 3.5-inch target. McMinn put all five shots in an area a little larger than a quarter and won the match. After that, if others found out he was entered in a competition, they would drop out because they knew he would win. The gun he is holding is a muzzle-loader made to his specifications. He walked from Carmichaels to Bruceton Mills, West Virginia, about 45 miles away, to place the order for the gun, and then later walked back to West Virginia to pick it up. McMinn nicknamed the gun "Old Benson" after the man who crafted it, M.M. Benson, who was known for turning out the best muzzle-loaders in the country west of the mountains. (Courtesy of Mabel McMinn.)

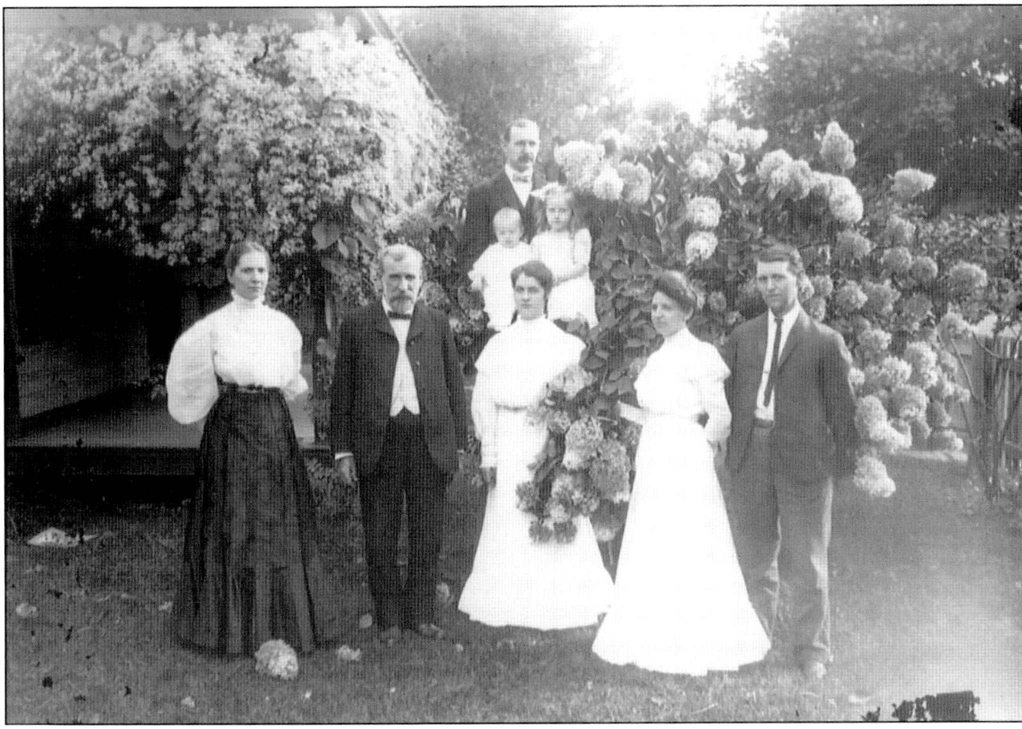

George W. Pennington and his family owned and operated the Pennington Greenhouse in Old Town. This photograph was taken from a glass negative that was later identified as showing the Pennington family. (Courtesy of Greene Academy of Art.)

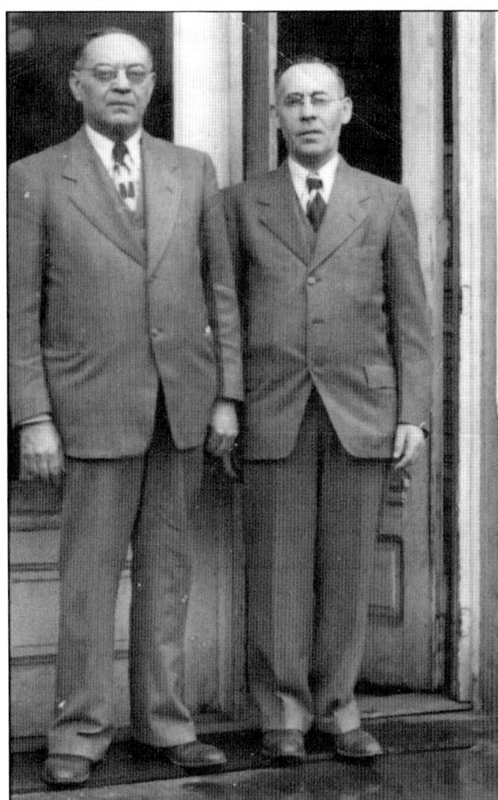

Pictured here are Paul Burger (left) and Sigmund Roth. Both men were very active in the community and opened the Carmichaels Department Store in 1919 when they purchased the G.W. Hewitt and Son Building on the town square. They ran the business until 1973. They believed in "one price only" as well as "cash only." (Courtesy of William Groves.)

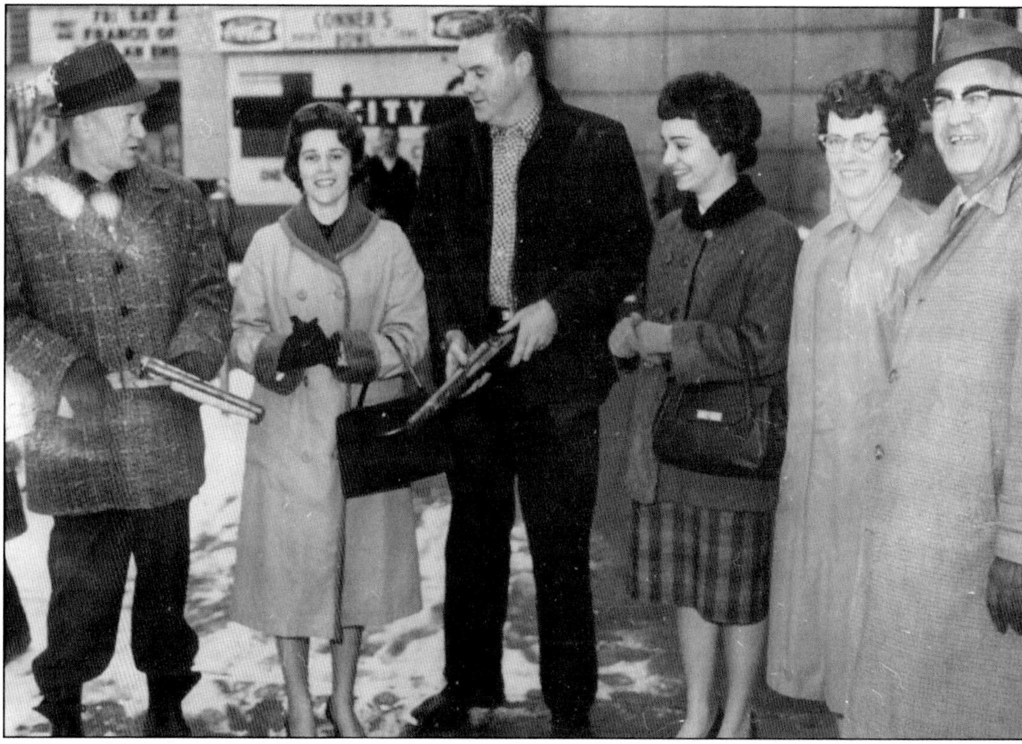

On December 1, 1961, the First National Bank of Carmichaels was held up by two robbers with sawed-off shotguns. The lookout, a third man, stayed outside the building. One of the robbers held a gun to the back of vice president Joe Dell, while the teller filled a bag with money. Pictured here are, from left to right, an FBI agent holding one of the shotguns used in the robbery, JoAnne Kline Baily, another FBI agent, Wilma Baker Allison, Donna Milak Rathburn, and Sergeant Rock. (Courtesy of Donna Milak Rathburn.)

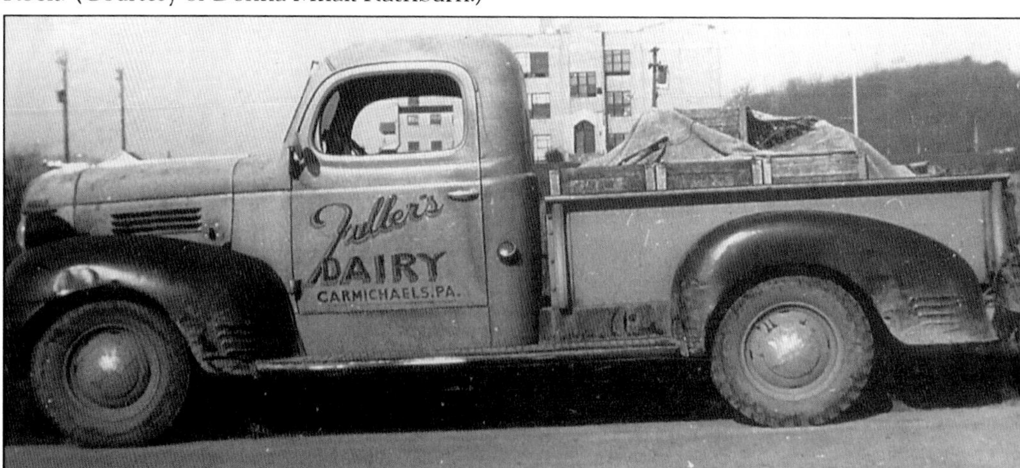

Bottled milk was kept cool at Fuller's Dairy by placing it in the spring water inside a springhouse. The milk was loaded onto a horse-drawn wagon for deliveries twice a day. Later, Ben Fuller converted a Model T Ford into a truck, which his business eventually outgrew. Pictured here is one of his trucks sitting on Greene Street in front of the Carmichaels–Cumberland Township High School. (Courtesy of the Donald W. Fuller family.)

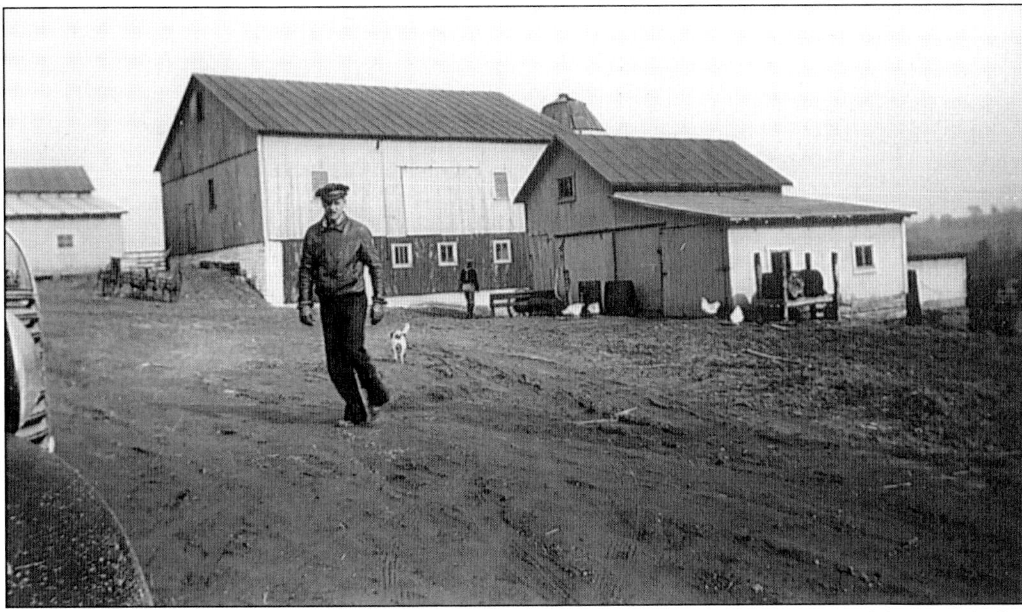

Pictured is the Fuller's Dairy farm, which began in 1916 on a Jacob's Ferry Road farm with five cows. From 1918 to 1942, the herd grew to 60 cows. Ben Fuller and his wife, Margaret, had three children, John, Ross, and Dorothy, who assisted in the daily operation of the dairy. The man in the photograph is unidentified. (Courtesy of Donald W. Fuller family.)

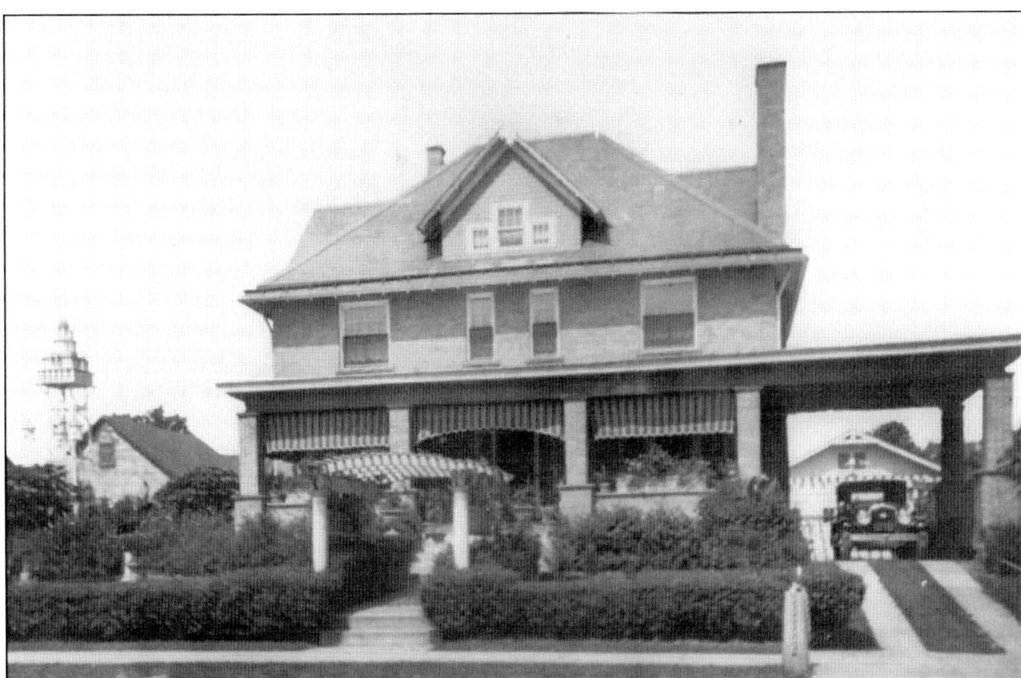

Pictured is the Flenniken Memorial Library on East George Street when it was the private residence of William H. and Elizabeth (Provins) Kerr. (Courtesy of Nelson Gideon.)

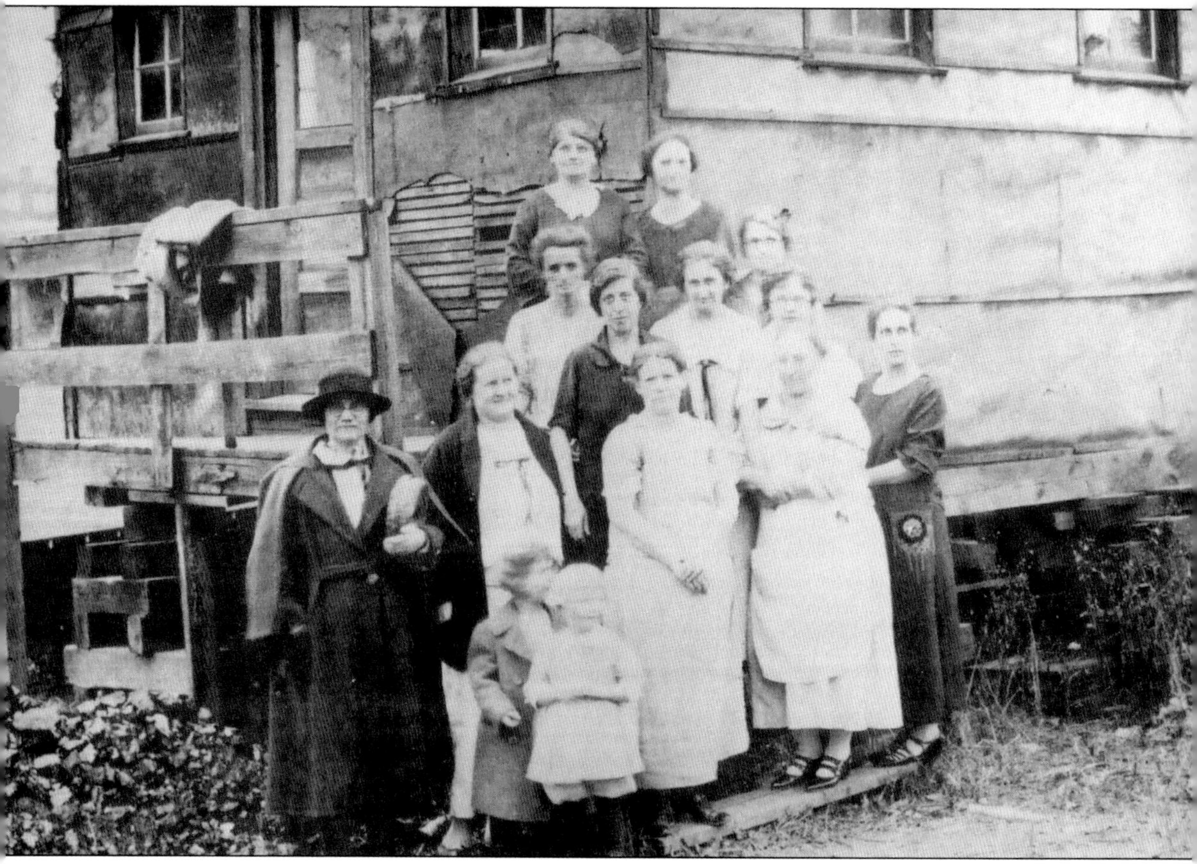

Pictured here are nurses and the building that was erected in Nemacolin in 24 hours. The coal miners of the Nemacolin Mine built the building to handle the overflow of patients during the Spanish Flu epidemic in 1918. It was equipped with steam heat. This temporary hospital was in the location where the elementary school was later built. The first hospital Nemacolin built, which was completed on May 1, 1918, was equipped to handle x-rays and major surgeries and had two nurses on continuous duty. This hospital was completed 12 years prior to the Greene County Memorial Hospital in Waynesburg. (Courtesy of Brice and Linda Rush and the Robert Korcheck collection.)

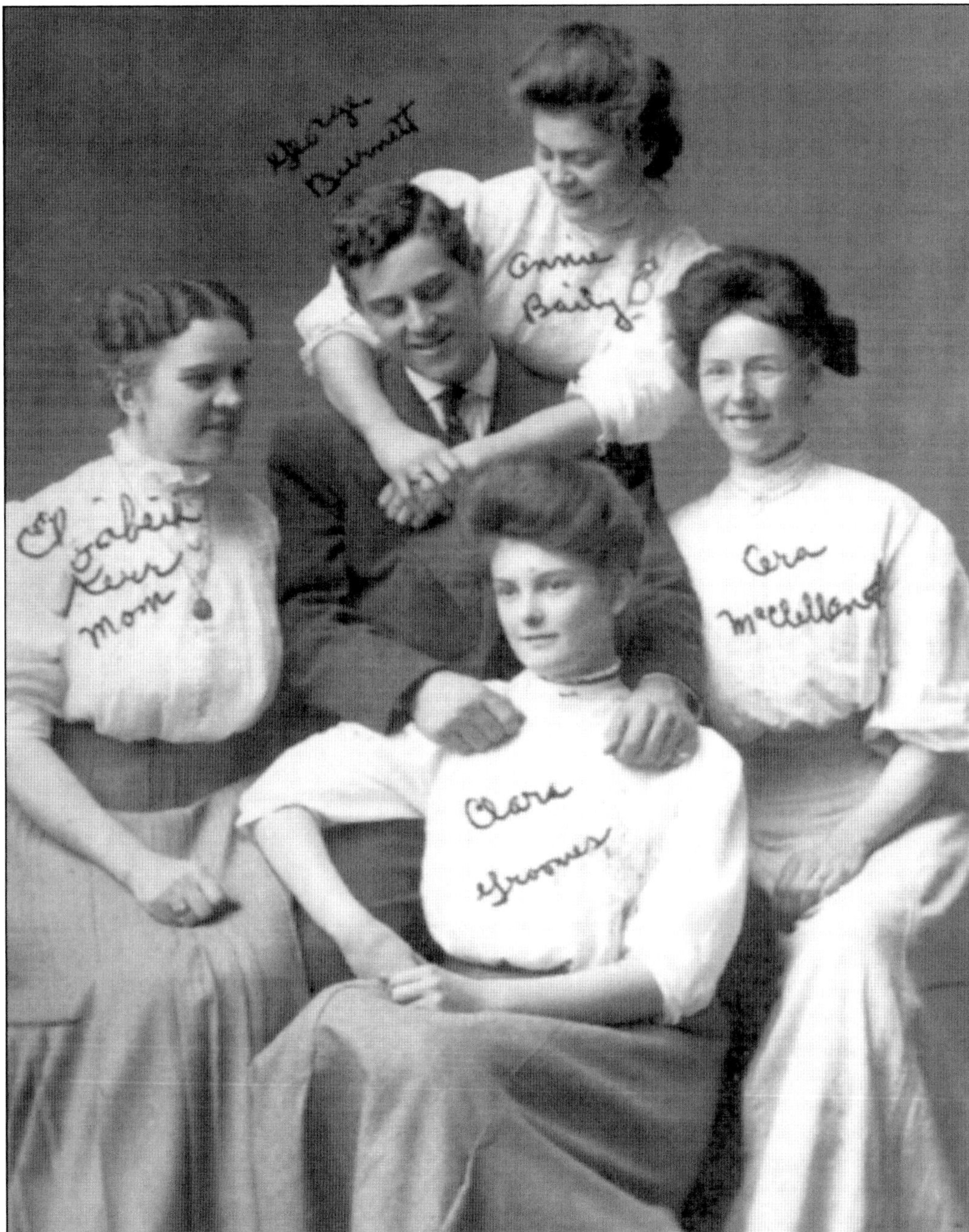

The first telephone operators used a hand crank to operate a generator to place phone calls. Pictured are George Burnette, Annie Baily, Ora McClelland, Clara Groomes, and Elizabeth (Provins) Kerr. Other early operators were Sara Long, Robert Lincoln, Ella Scott, Mary McClelland, Pearl Rinehart, Anna Barkman, Grant Barclay, Alice Miller, and Bessie Crago. (Courtesy of Amy [Kerr] Gideon.)

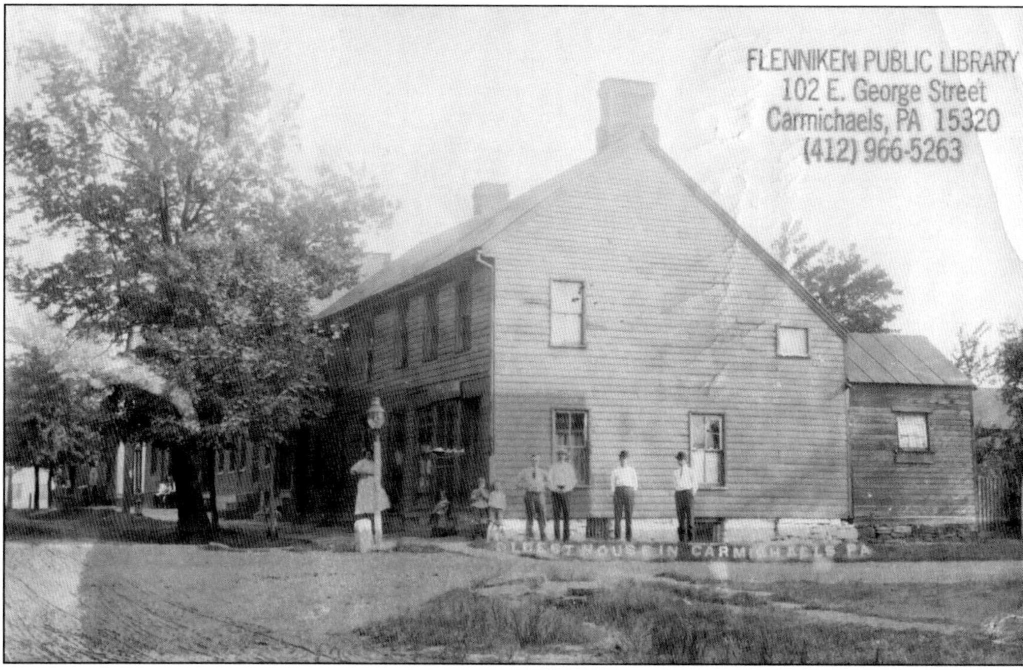

William "Billy" Lincoln owned the house located at the corner of West Greene and North Market Streets; it was believed to have been among the oldest log cabin buildings in the area. The home was demolished in 1965 for the construction of the post office. (Courtesy of Flenniken Memorial Library.)

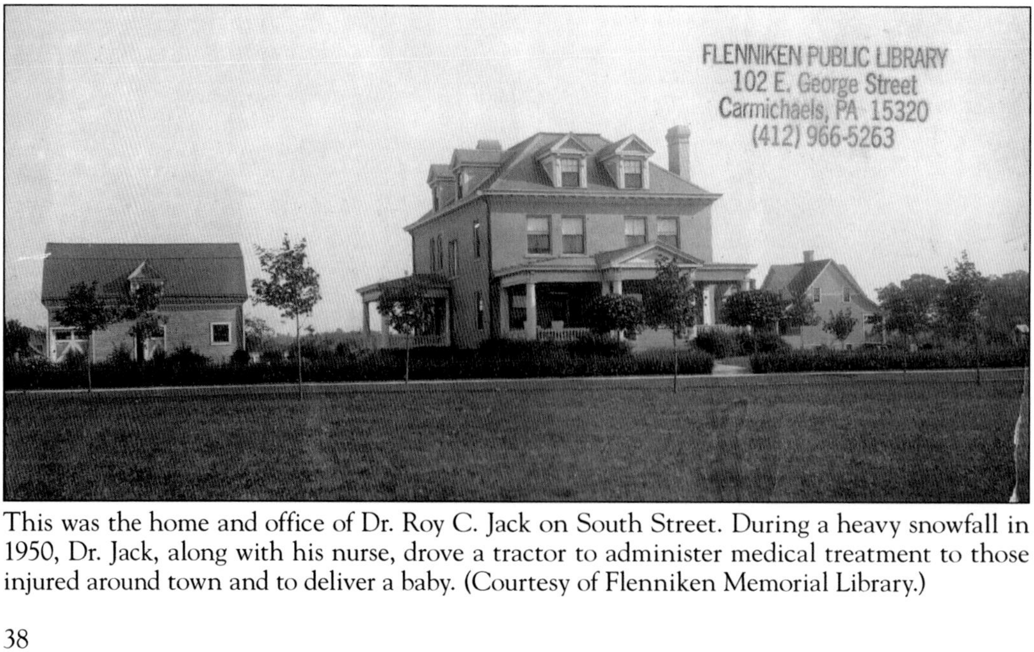

This was the home and office of Dr. Roy C. Jack on South Street. During a heavy snowfall in 1950, Dr. Jack, along with his nurse, drove a tractor to administer medical treatment to those injured around town and to deliver a baby. (Courtesy of Flenniken Memorial Library.)

Dr. Andrew J. Gibbons purchased a one-and-a-half-story home on the corner of West George and Pine Streets, which he tore down to build a three-story building. This was the location of his office, some hospital rooms, and living quarters for him and his family. In later years, the building was used as apartments, and although numerous attempts were made to keep and preserve this beautiful historic building, it was eventually torn down. (Courtesy of Carole Gideon.)

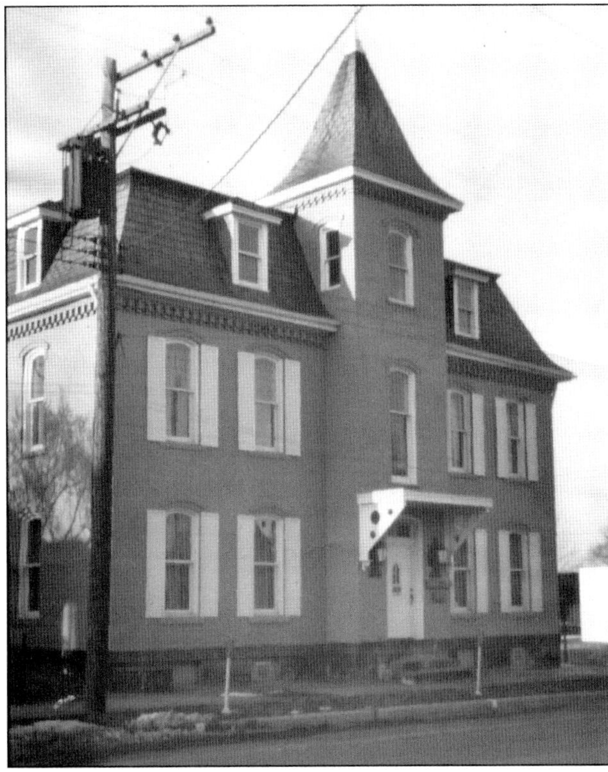

Pictured here is Jesse James Sanner, a well-remembered resident of Old Town, pointing to the sign showing when Old Town was founded in 1767. It was the first settlement in Cumberland Township in Greene County (formerly Washington County). (Courtesy of Todd and Lisa Allison.)

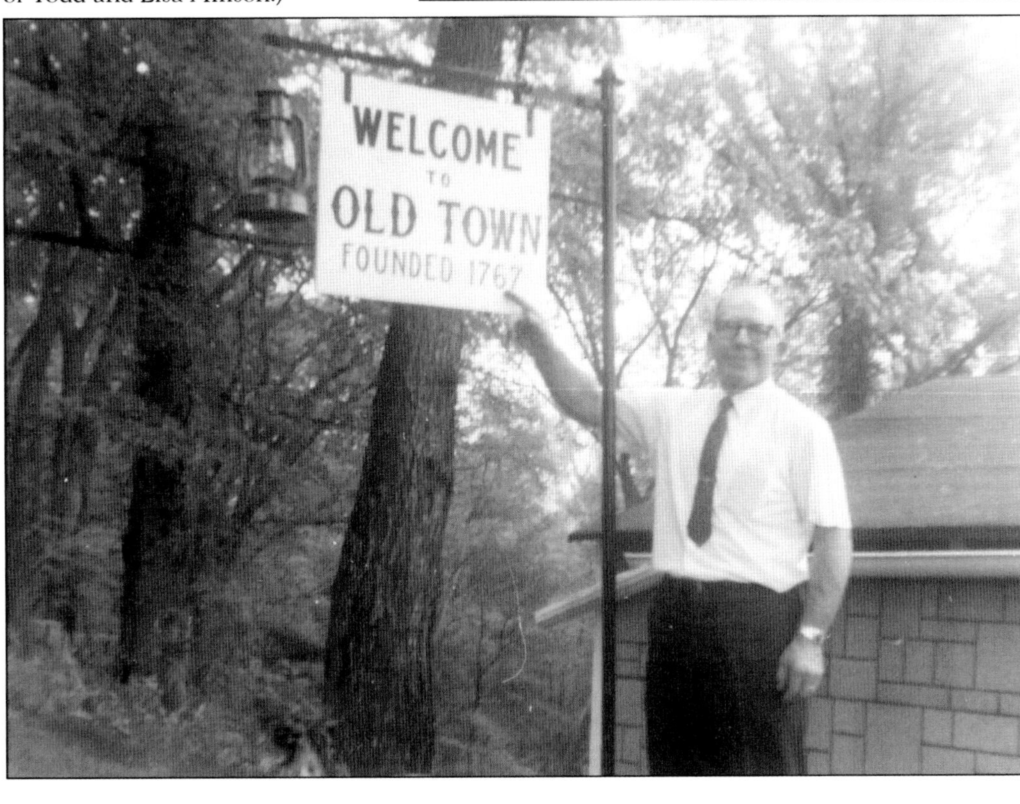

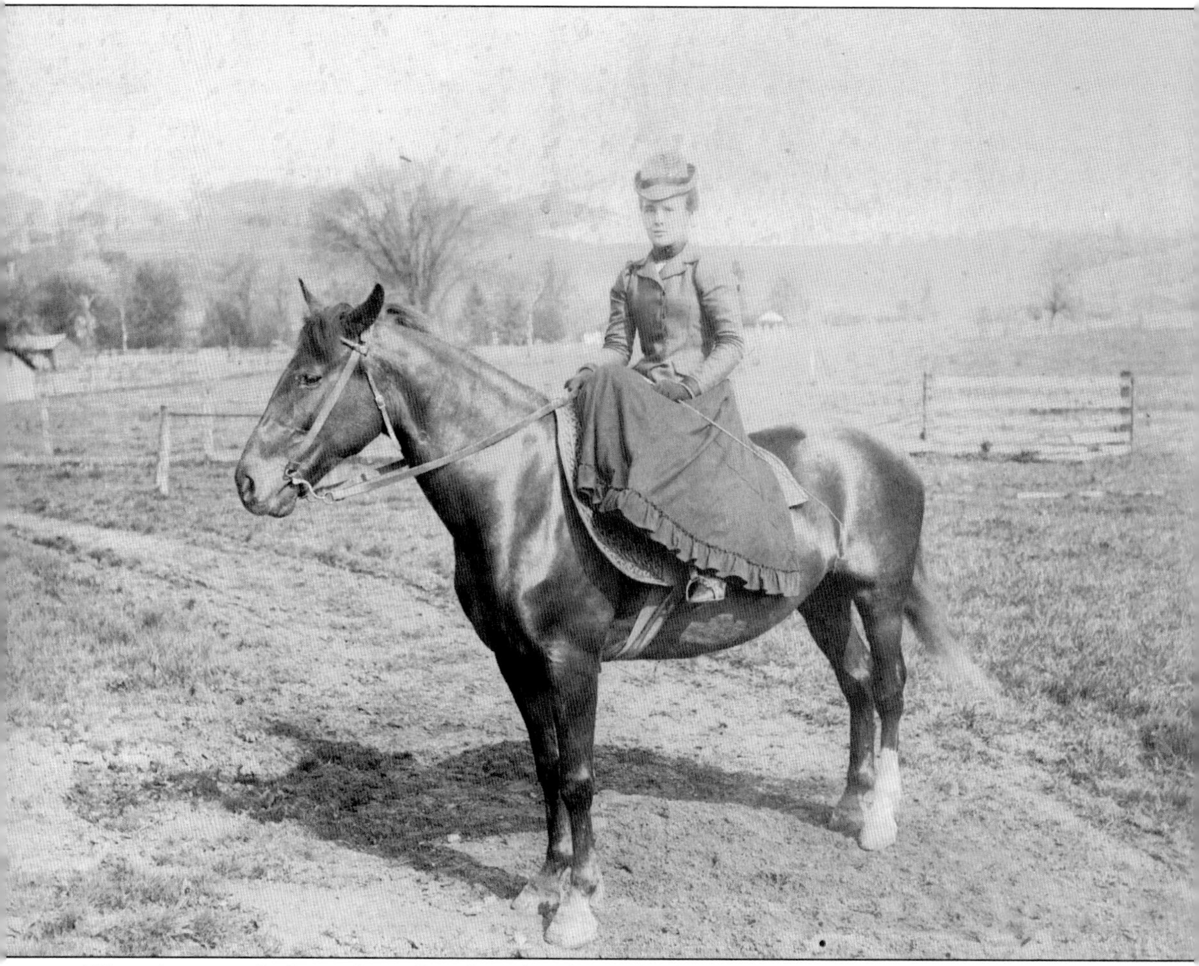

This photograph shows Lena Dowlin, daughter of John Dowlin, on her horse Nellie. Nellie pulled a buckboard, driven by John Dowlin, to the Farmers and Drovers Bank in Waynesburg on July 1, 1901, to pick up the cash to open the First National Bank of Carmichaels. (Courtesy of William Groves.)

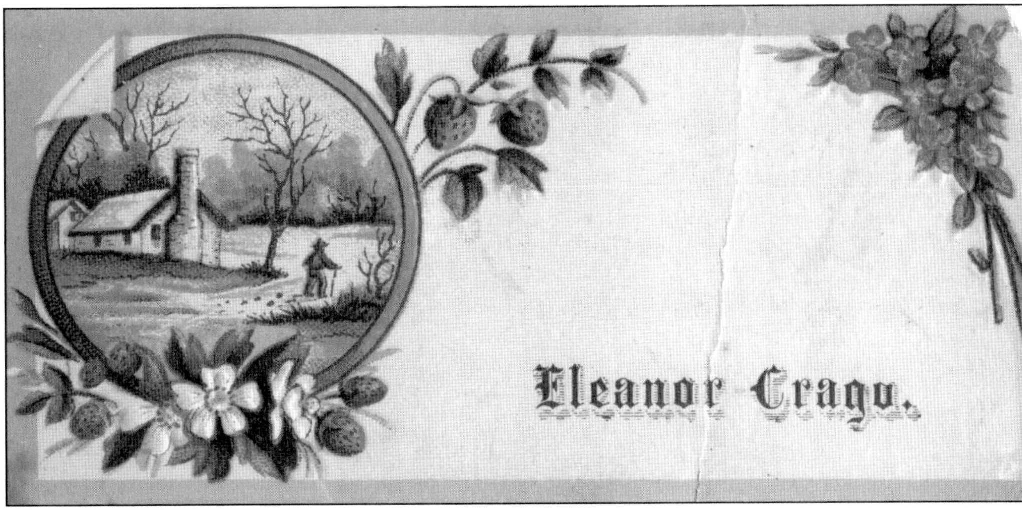

Calling cards began in France in the early 1800s and became popular in the United States between 1840 and 1900. The calling card was a social custom and a cherished and highly skilled craft of calligraphy and embellishment. Different styles, designs, and colors reflected different messages. Men as well as women carried calling cards. This card belonged to Eleanor (Flenniken) Crago, wife of John B. Crago and daughter of John and Mary (McClelland) Flenniken. (Courtesy of Lenny McMinn.)

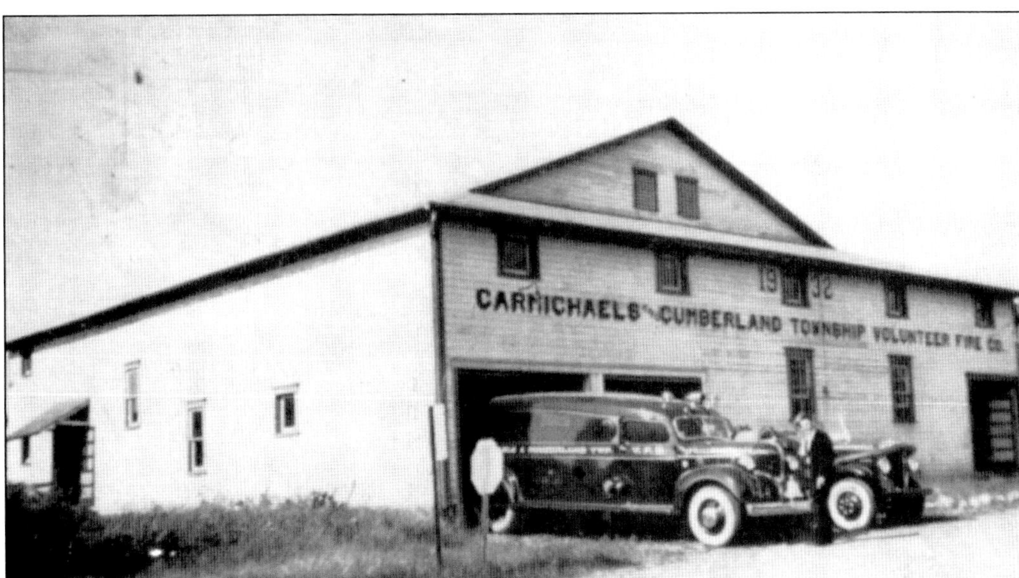

This building housed the Carmichaels–Cumberland Township Volunteer Fire Company on West George Street in 1932. The first volunteer fire company was formed in 1923 and was named the Carmichaels Volunteer Fire Company. Other records for that same year indicate that the name was to be the Cumberland Volunteer Fire Department of Carmichaels. On November 26, 1929, a motion was passed to change the name of the fire company to Carmichaels–Cumberland Township Volunteer Fire Company. (Courtesy of Carole Gideon.)

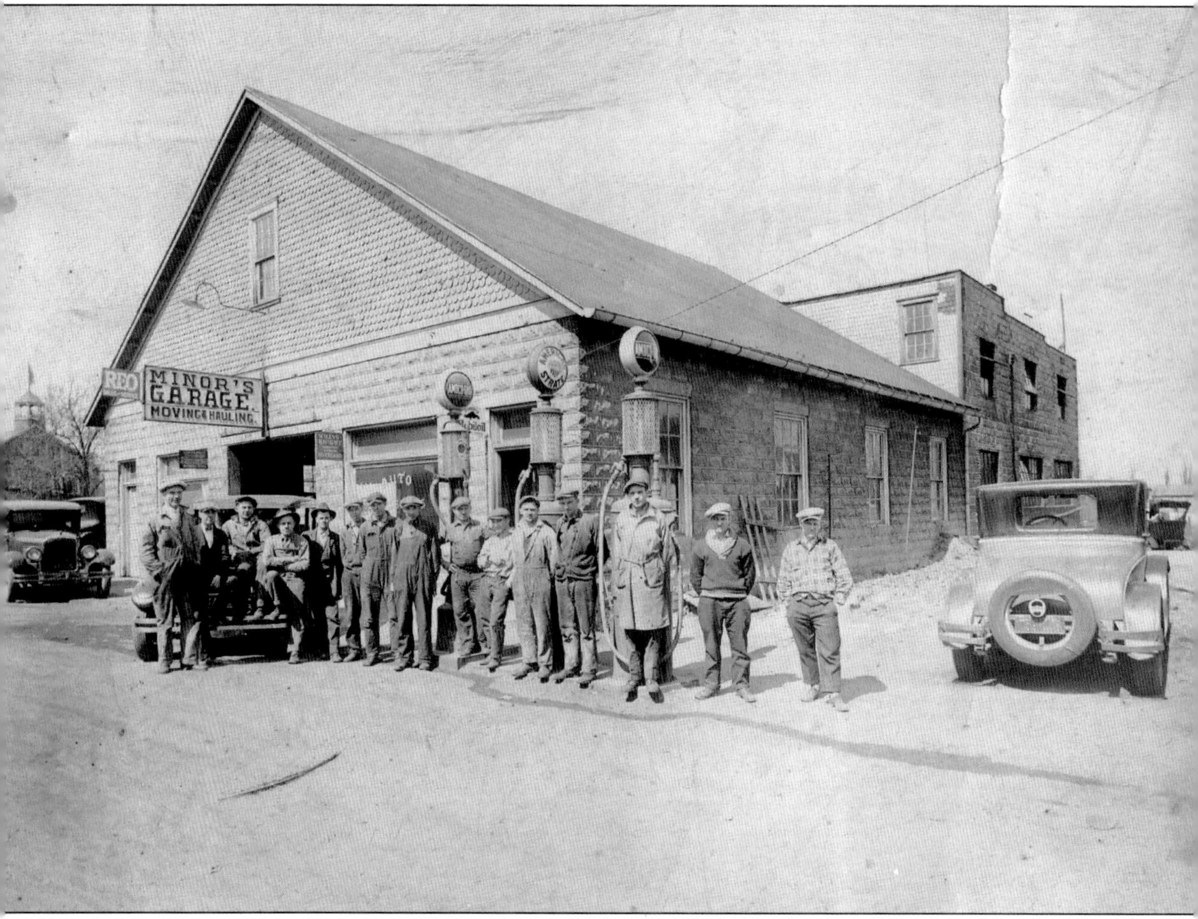

This picture shows a group of men outside Minor's Garage on Pine Street. The garage was built by Pearson Minor. In 1912, the dealership sold Hudson automobiles. At one time, there were 15 men working at the garage, including Claude Smith and George Mt. Joy. Minor's Garage was open from 1911 to 1933. (Courtesy of Greene Academy of Art.)

Three

A Walk around the Town

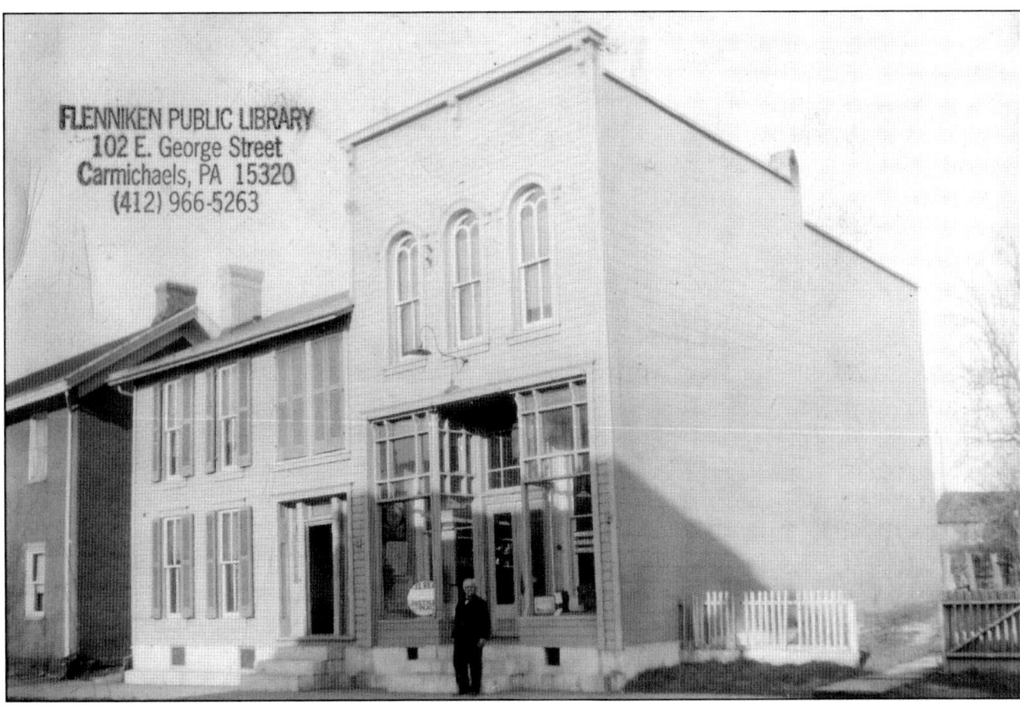

This building was once the home and business of Albert M. Richey, which later became the property of Justice of the Peace Jesse L. Rea (pictured). Richey had a furniture store, and his daughter Emma had a millinery shop. Emma would walk the streets selling her wares from a wheelbarrow, which had her name on the side. (Courtesy of Flenniken Memorial Library.)

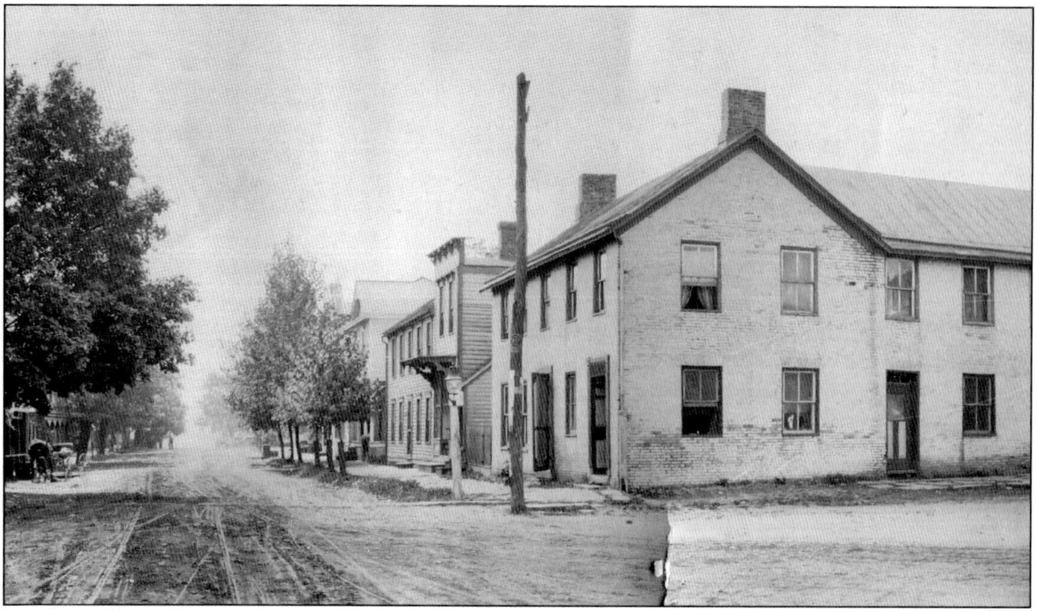

Pictured here is what was later referred to as the Helen Minor Building. In the mid-1800s, Alfred Frost owned this building, which was his home. There was a storeroom on the corner, which was used by Billy Donohoe, a shoemaker. Alfred Frost's daughter Mary lived here for many years prior to her death. (Courtesy of Greene County Historical Society and Museum.)

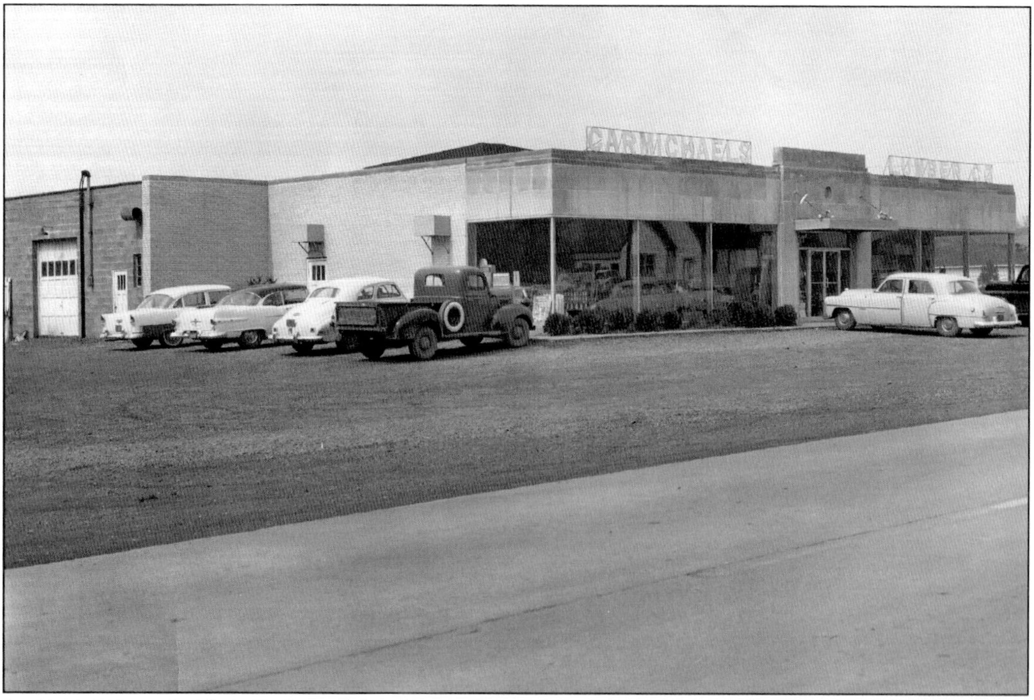

In 1948, Edgar Gabler purchased the Carmichaels Lumber Company from Earl T. Flenniken. At that time, the lumber company was located at 204 South Pine Street. A few years later, Gabler built this building at 434 West George Street and received an award for Most Outstanding Building for a Lumber Yard in the United States. (Courtesy of Norma Gabler Kline.)

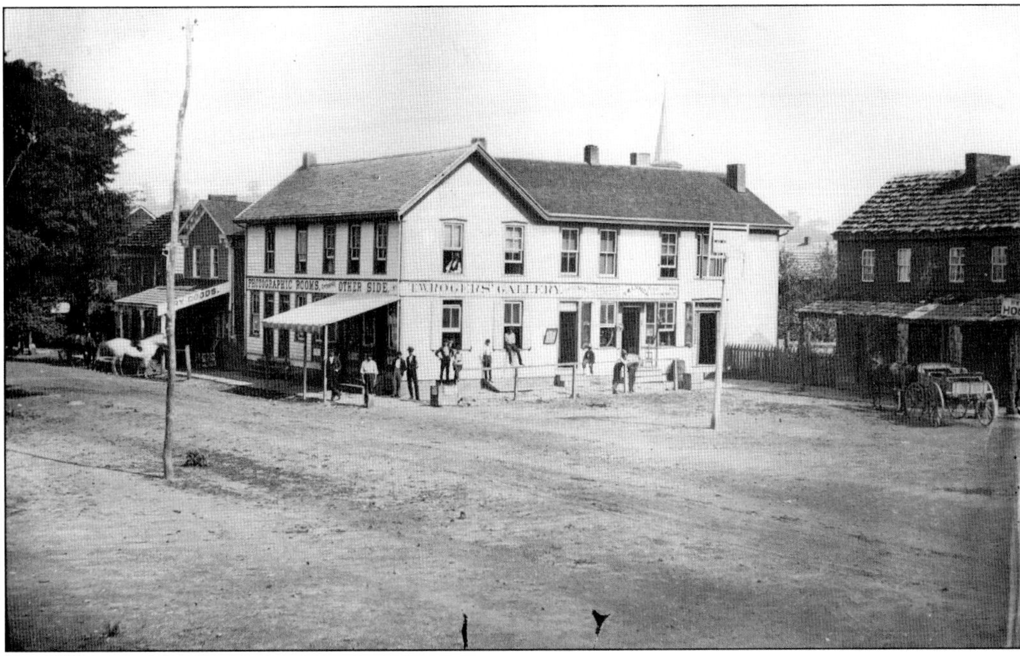

This 1874 photograph shows the Ross Building, better known as the Rogers Portrait Studio. Many local photographs still bear the name of T.W. Rogers. In 1910, this building caught on fire and burned to the ground, along with five others. To the right of the Ross Building was the Smith house, also known as the Red Tavern. (Courtesy of Greene Academy of Art.)

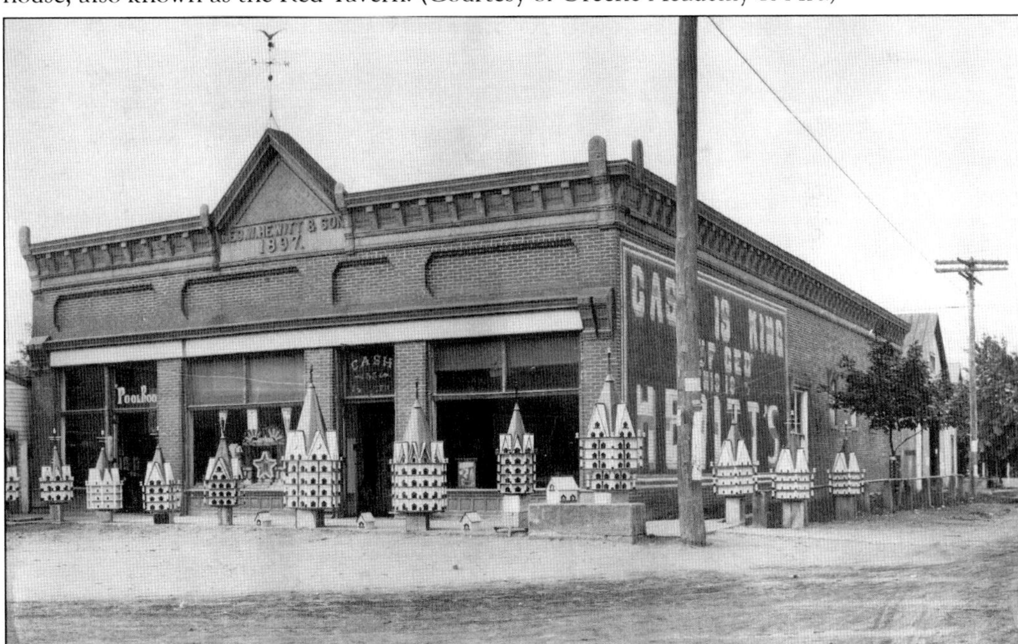

In 1897, George W. Hewitt and Son constructed this building on the town square. Hewitt hauled all the bricks used in the building from the John Bailey farm with a pony and wagon. The building was the first one with a street-level entrance. (Courtesy of Greene County Historical Society and Museum.)

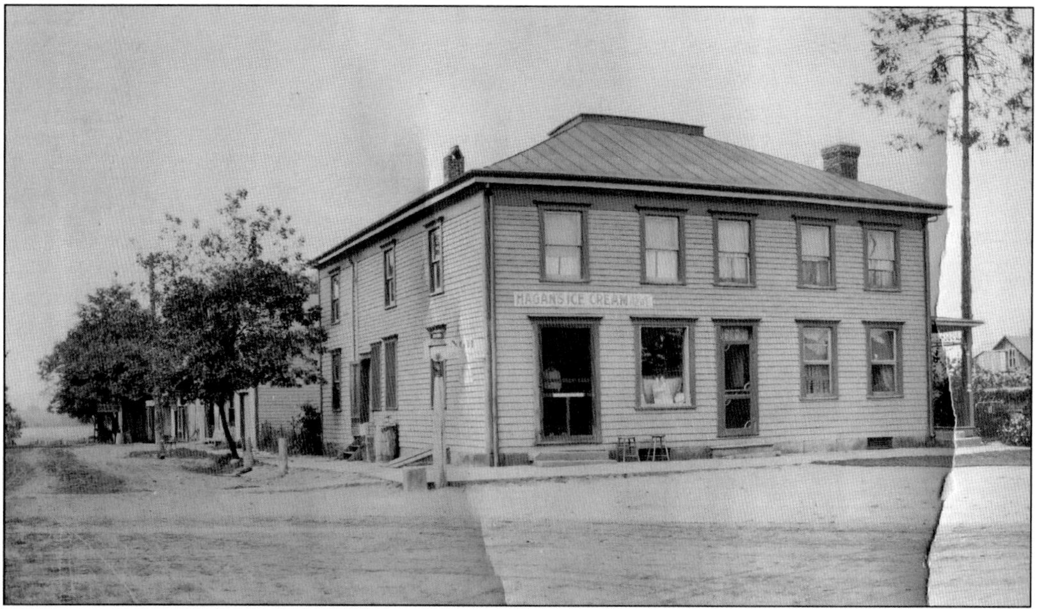

In 1923, Glenn J. Darrah purchased this building and opened a restaurant featuring fresh seafood from Baltimore, Maryland. It also featured a soda fountain serving Hagen's Ice Cream. The restaurant closed in 1927. (Courtesy of Greene County Historical Society and Museum.)

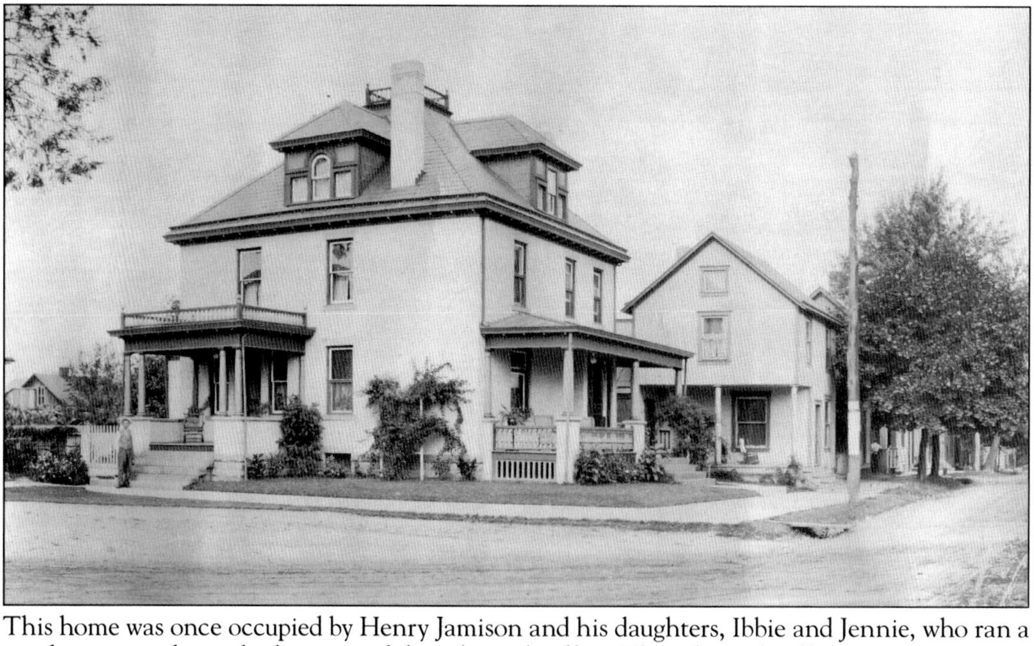

This home was once occupied by Henry Jamison and his daughters, Ibbie and Jennie, who ran a candy store, and was the location of the telegraph office. The telegraph office was in operation as late as 1905. Jennie Jamison taught some young men how to send and receive messages. On one Sunday morning in 1898, one of these young men dropped into Jennie Jamison's office, and while he was there, the message of Dewey's victory at Manila Bay came over the wire. The young man "stole" the message, and soon, the quiet of a Sabbath morning was broken by a fife and drum band, which the young man had hastily gotten together to celebrate Dewey's victory—surely a first for Carmichaels. (Courtesy of Greene County Historical Society and Museum.)

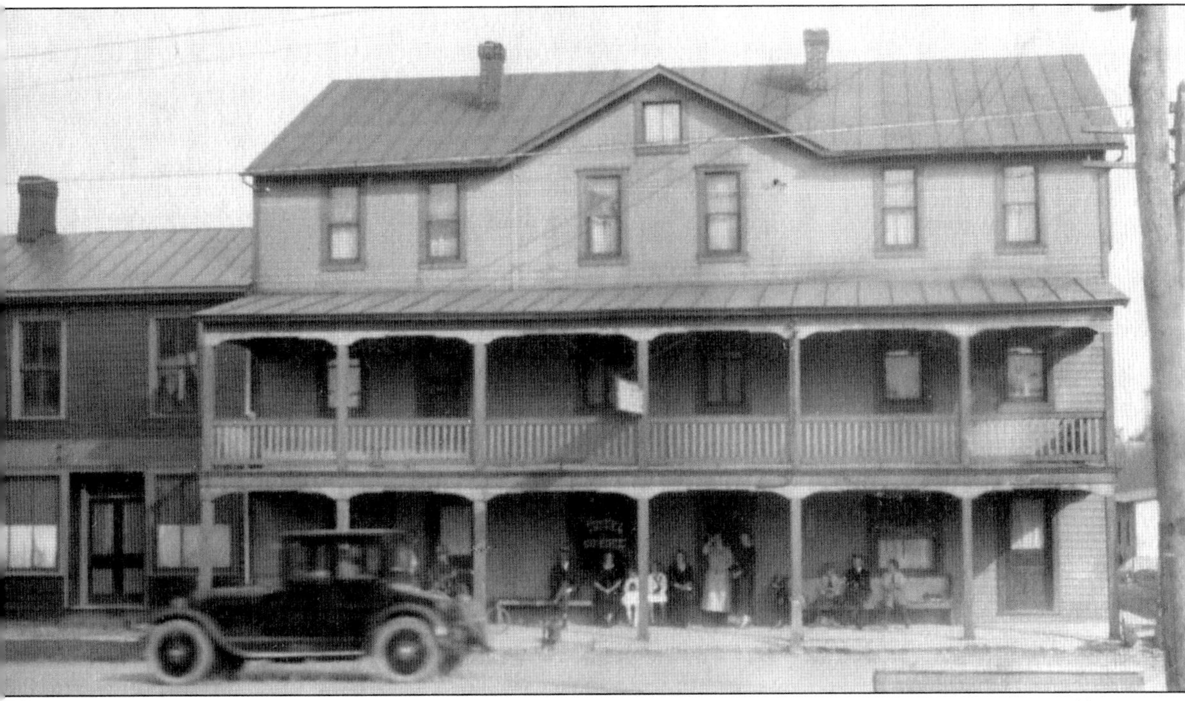

This is the Home Hotel, built in 1895 by James B. Schroyer. Proprietor Lewis N. Burnette and his family ran the hotel with two other staff members. Behind the hotel was a livery stable and barn. The hotel contained a large parlor and dining room, and was the headquarters of the Tri-State Fox Hunters Association. (Courtesy of Greene County Historical Society and Museum.)

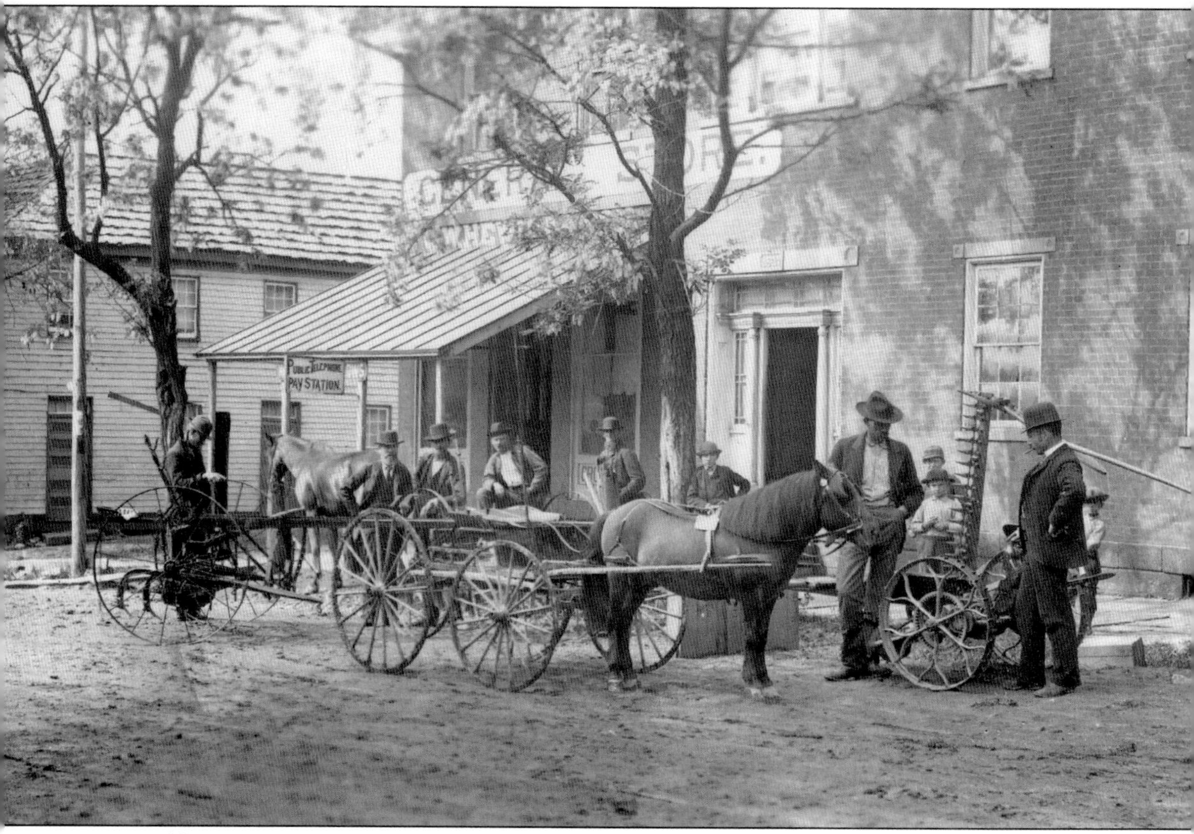

Pictured here is a two-story redbrick building at the corner of North Market and Greene Streets, directly across from the current post office. George W. Hewitt once had a general store in this building, which in later years became known as the Hathaway Building. John W. Hathaway had his first general store in this building, which had a courtyard in the back. After his death in 1887, his son Charles Yard Hathaway took over the business, which then went to his son Lynn Hathaway, who operated it until 1938. After that time the building served various purposes, such as an electric shop, restaurant, and apartments. (Courtesy of Greene County Historical Society and Museum.)

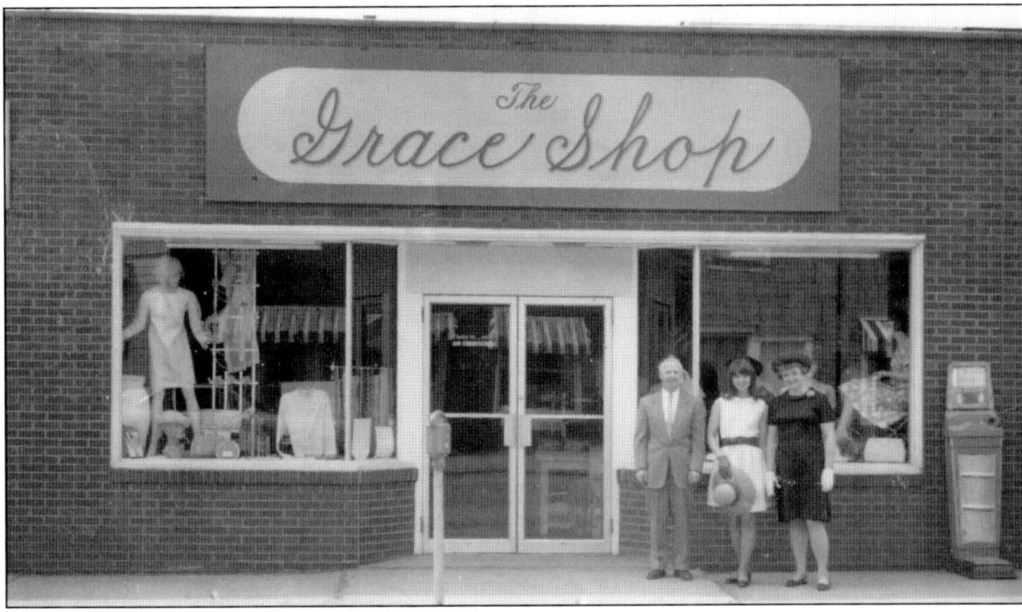

Pictured here is Joseph and Grace Harkins and their daughter Christine in front of the Grace Shop. This was a women's clothing store that operated from 1957 to 1977, when Joseph and Grace retired. They turned the business over to Christine and her husband, Edward Walko, who ran it as Edward's Department Store. (Courtesy of Flenniken Memorial Library.)

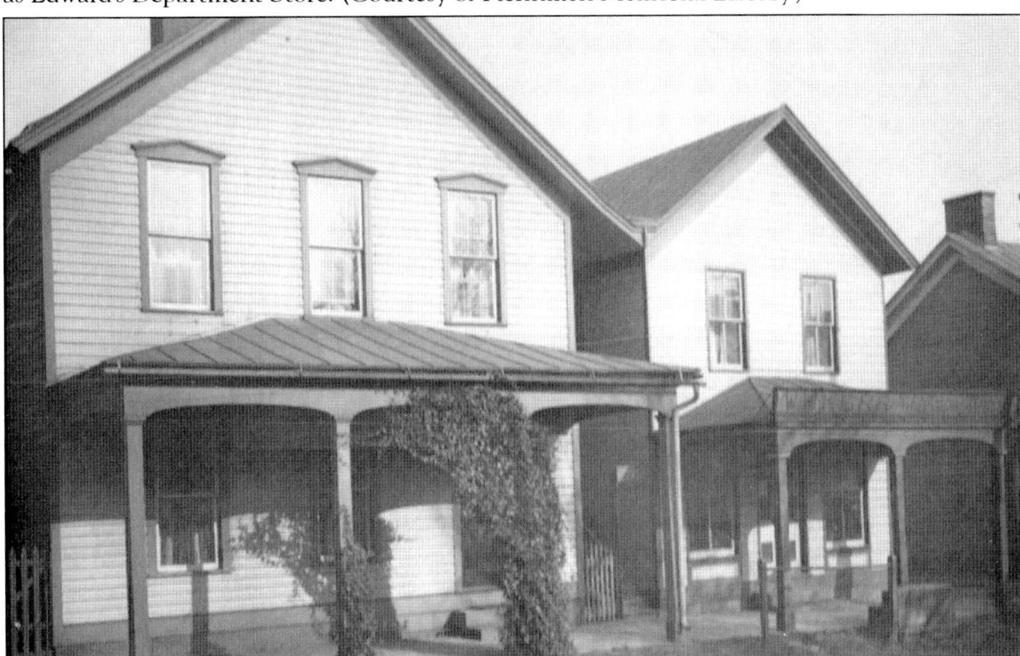

William H. Kerr first purchased the building on the right and opened a general store. He later purchased the building on the left, expanding his business. The business was later taken over by his daughter and son-in-law, Amy and George Gideon, and was in operation for 44 years. Later, their son Nelson Kerr Gideon and his wife, Marianne (Prodan) Gideon, operated a home improvement store there until his death in 2009. (Courtesy of Brice and Linda Rush.)

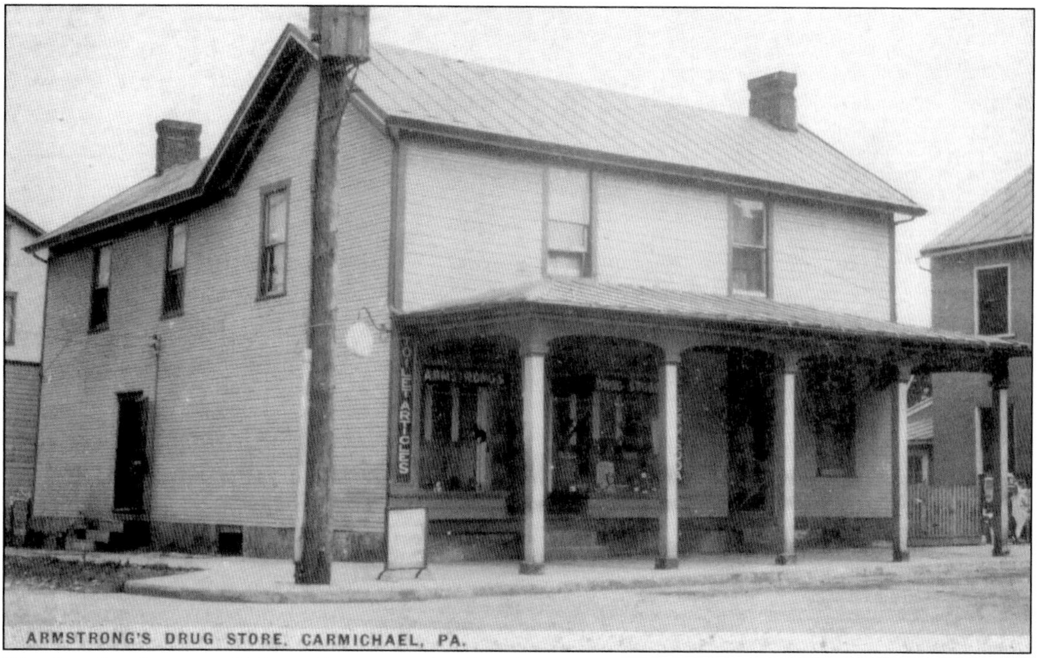

The Laidley Boot and Shoe Shop was the first business to operate in this building. Eventually, the shop was sold to Neri Armstrong, who opened a pharmacy around 1904. Armstrong lived in the rear of the building; later, his son Alfred took over the pharmacy, which he ran until 1950. (Courtesy of Carole Gideon.)

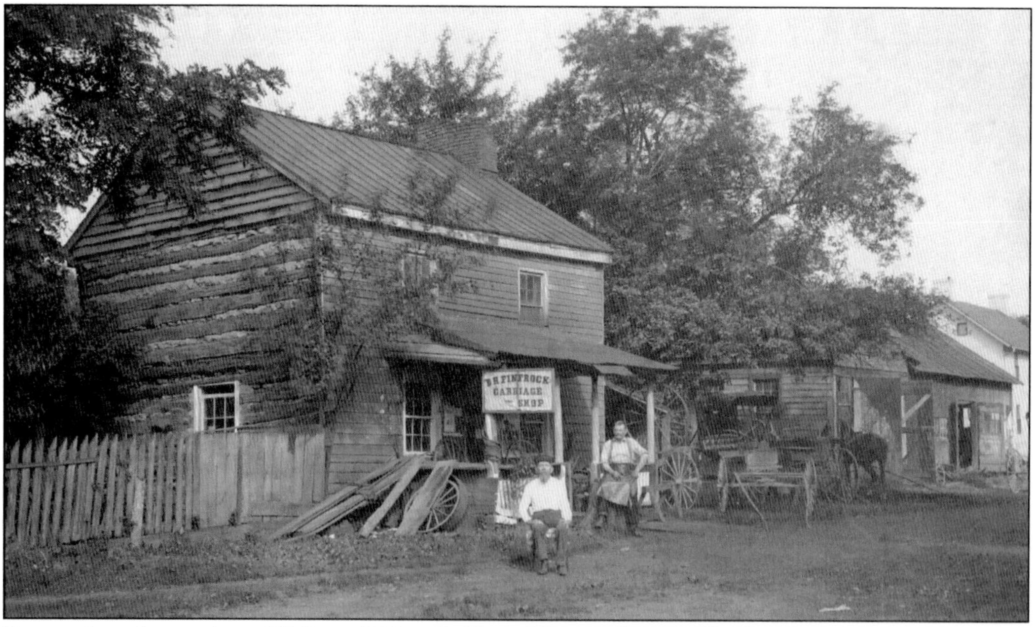

Pictured are horse-shoer William Wiley (left) and his nephew Millard F. "Lane" Hunnell at the Finfrock Carriage Shop and Blacksmith Shop. The blacksmith shop was located in the triangle between South Street, Market Street, and Morgantown Road, facing Market Street. The only two families to ever use the carriage shop as a home were Millard Hunnell and John Helmick. (Courtesy of William Groves.)

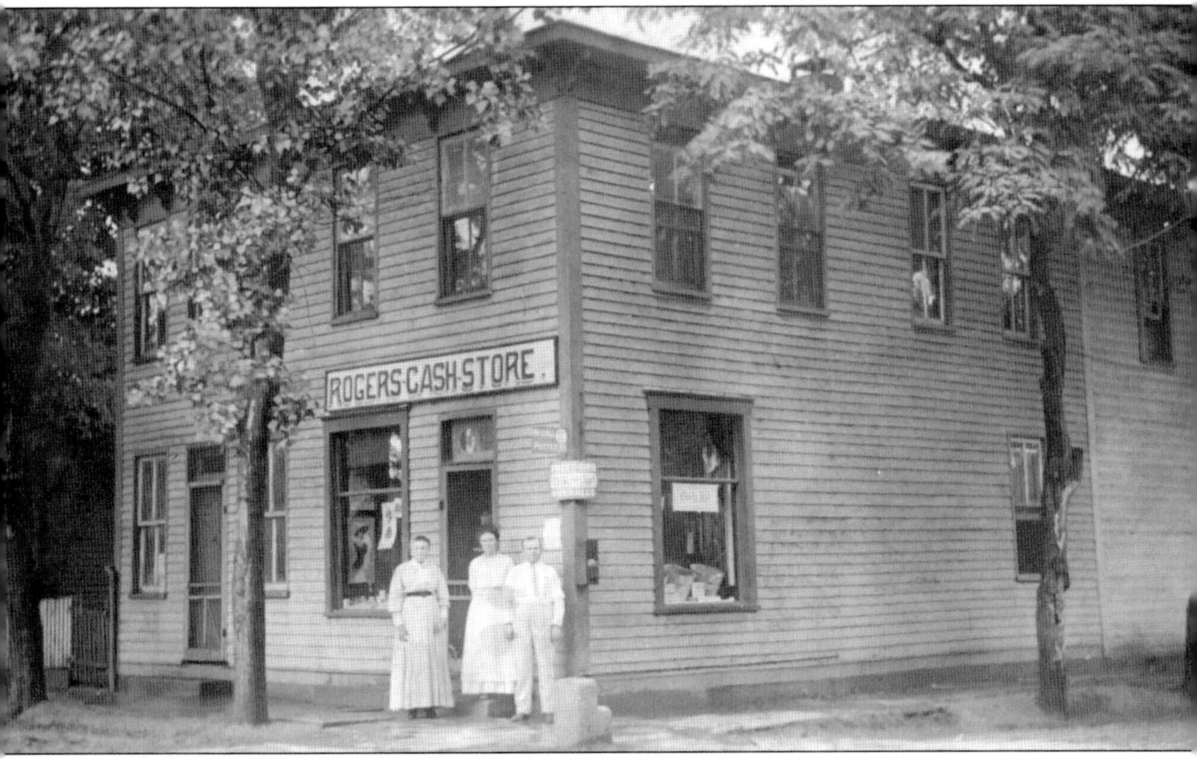

Rogers Cash Store is remembered for selling penny candy, McCall's patterns, and other general merchandise. It was located at the corner of North Market and Greene Streets, and was later torn down and replaced by a redbrick building. (Courtesy of Joyce Fortney.)

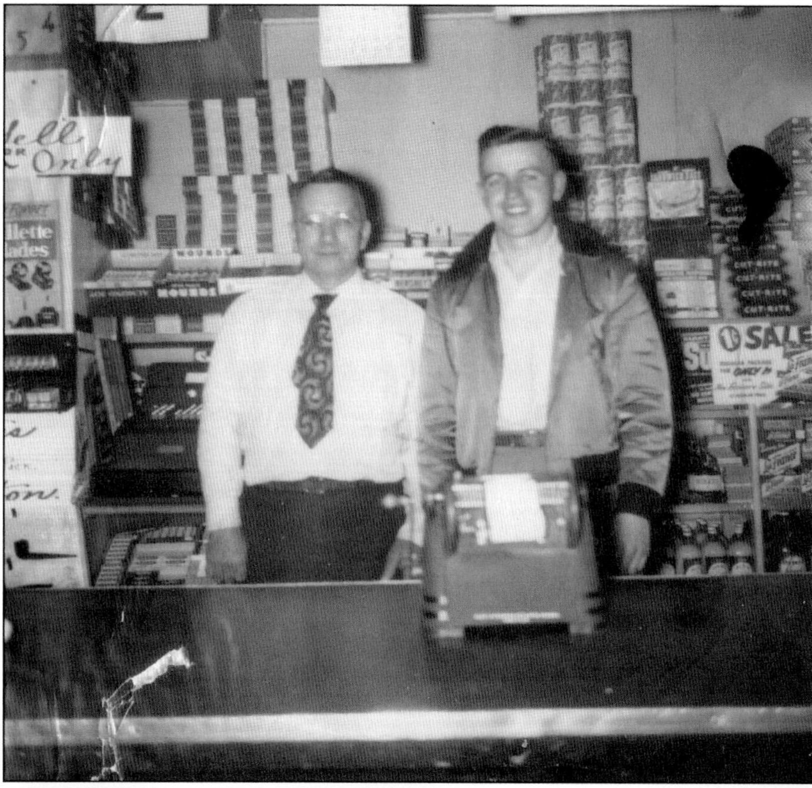

On the left is George P. Gideon, son-in-law of William H. and Elizabeth (Provins) Kerr, who assumed management of Kerr's Model Store. On the right is one of the store's employees, Walter Gareth McMinn, a cousin of George. (Courtesy of Carole Gideon.)

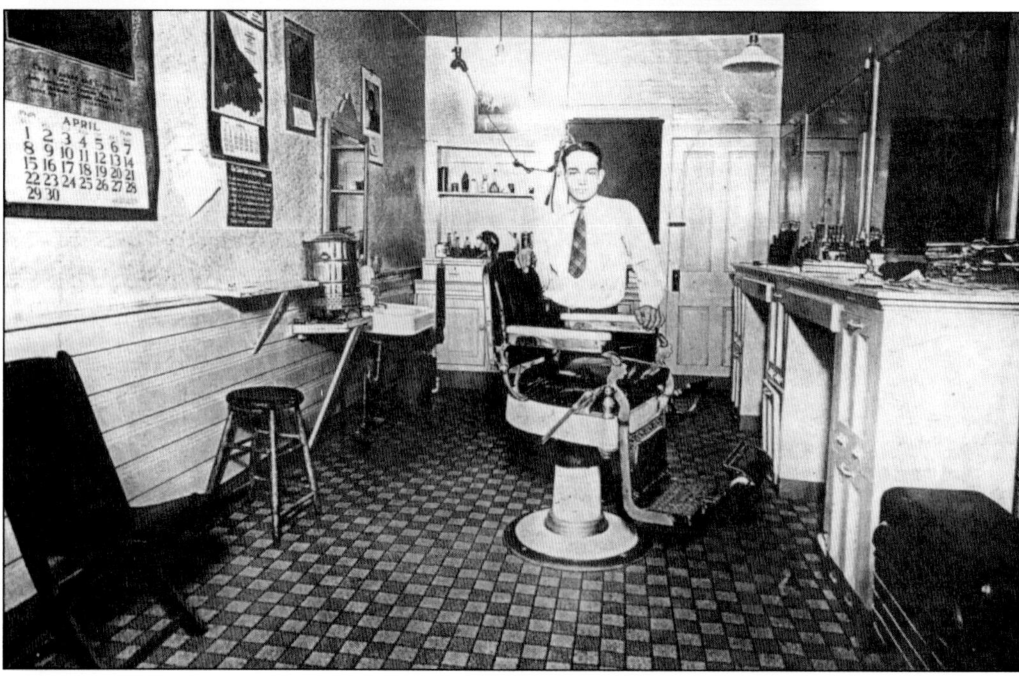

Although it was reported that Paul Miller was a barber in Carmichaels from 1927 until his death in 1968, the calendar in this photograph bears the year 1924. During the 1950s, Miller was a barber-beauty shop inspector for Pennsylvania. (Courtesy of Flenniken Memorial Library.)

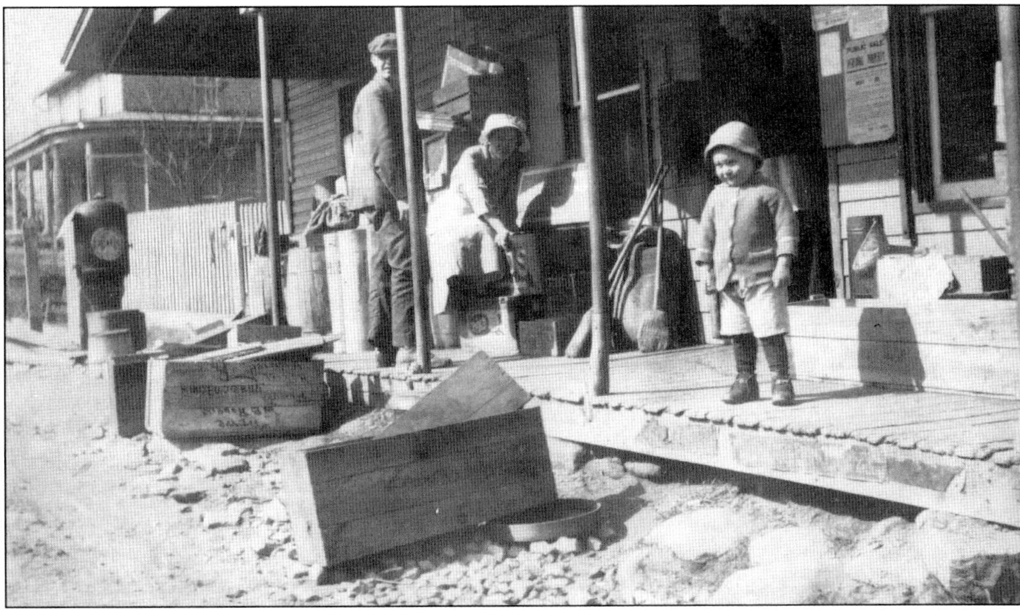

This lovely photograph shows what appears to be a family at a general store, which was marked as being in Carmichaels. The location and name of the store are unknown. (Courtesy of Greene County Historical Society and Museum.)

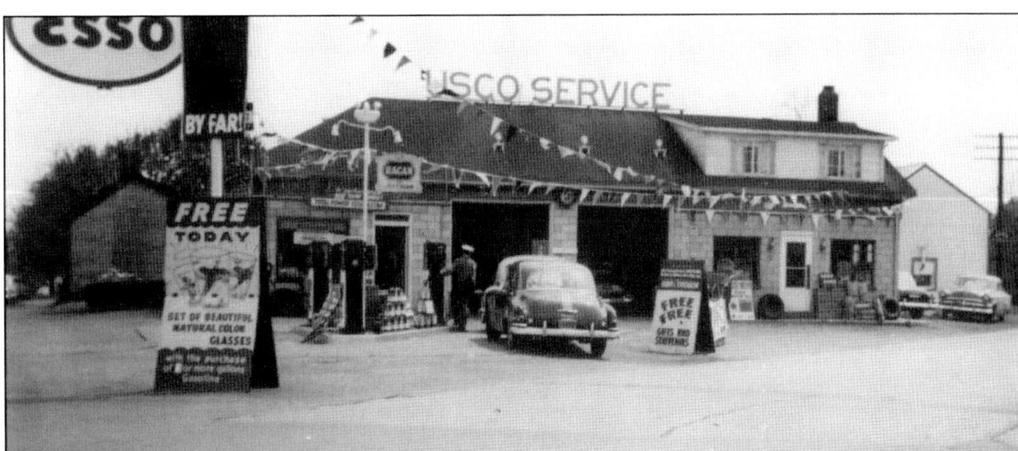

Note the sign for "USCO Service" on the roof. The Union Supply Company leased this service station in 1945 from Harold Sharpnack. The station changed ownership several times, but in 1959, Carl and Wilma Allison purchased the property. Carl Allison's nickname was Jum, and from 1959 until he retired, the service station was known as "Jum's." (Courtesy of Brice and Linda Rush.)

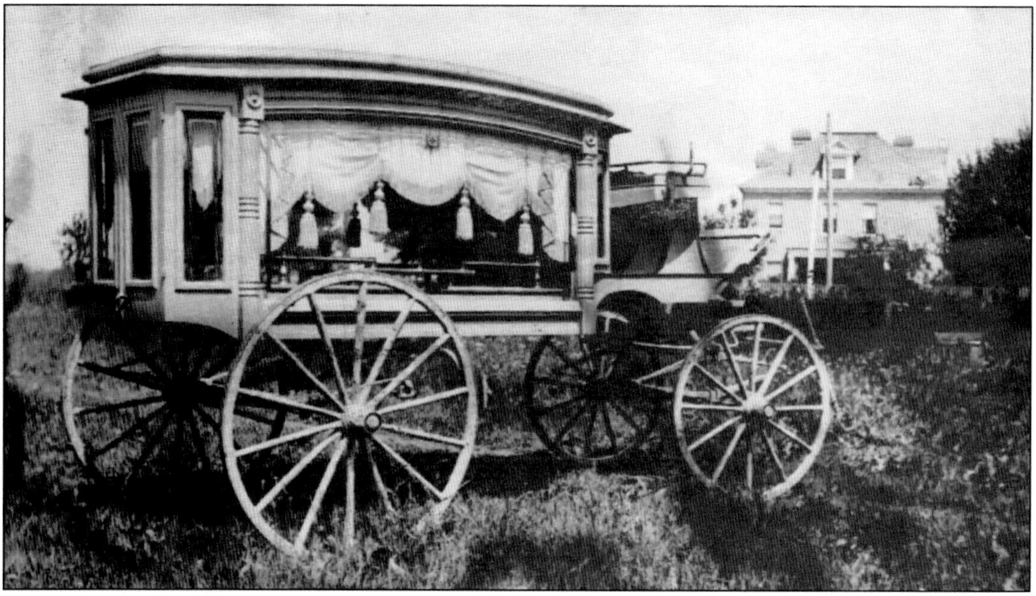

Pictured is the Condit Funeral Home hearse. George M. Condit and his son Walter were furniture makers and undertakers. Their business card, which had a wooden rocking chair in the middle, had the words "Furniture Making and Undertaking – Embalming a Specialty." This horse-drawn hearse was used into the early 1900s. (Courtesy of Paul M. Lesako.)

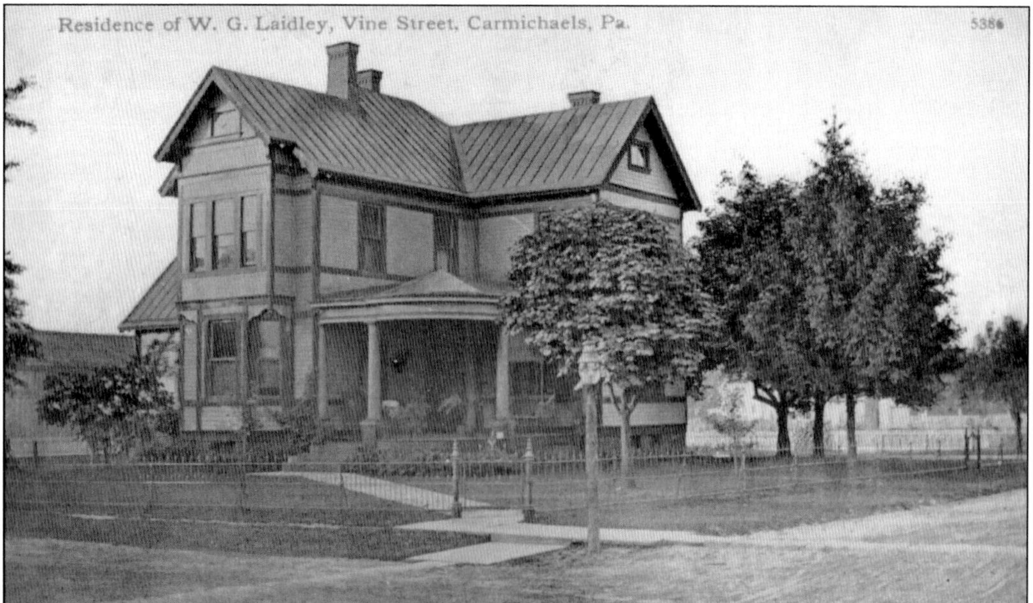

This beautiful house on the corner of South and South Vine Streets was once the home of W.G. Laidley. The property that this house was built on was once part of the estate of John Walton Hathaway. The house has been well taken care of over the years, and is still occupied. (Courtesy of Carole Gideon.)

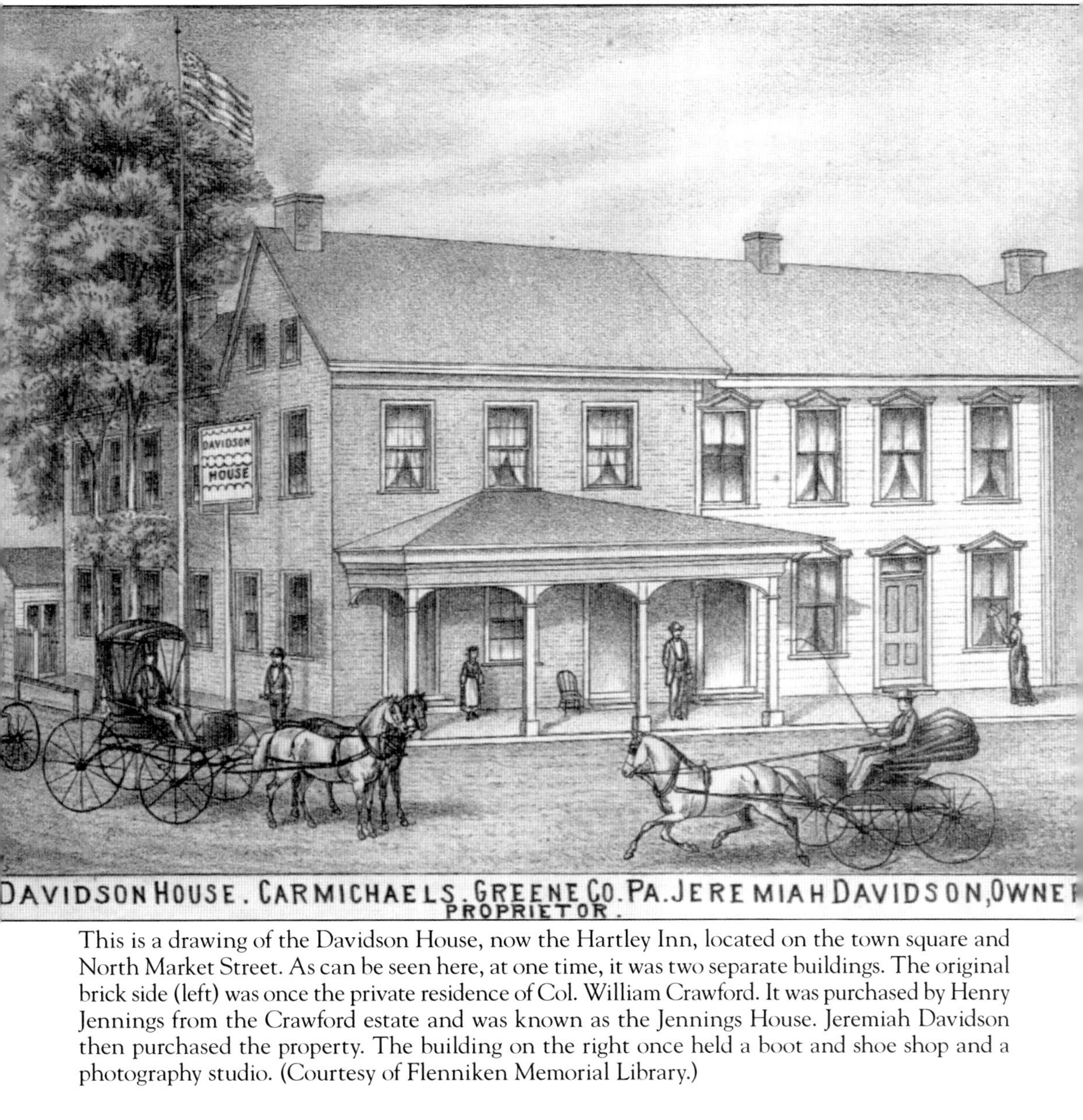

This is a drawing of the Davidson House, now the Hartley Inn, located on the town square and North Market Street. As can be seen here, at one time, it was two separate buildings. The original brick side (left) was once the private residence of Col. William Crawford. It was purchased by Henry Jennings from the Crawford estate and was known as the Jennings House. Jeremiah Davidson then purchased the property. The building on the right once held a boot and shoe shop and a photography studio. (Courtesy of Flenniken Memorial Library.)

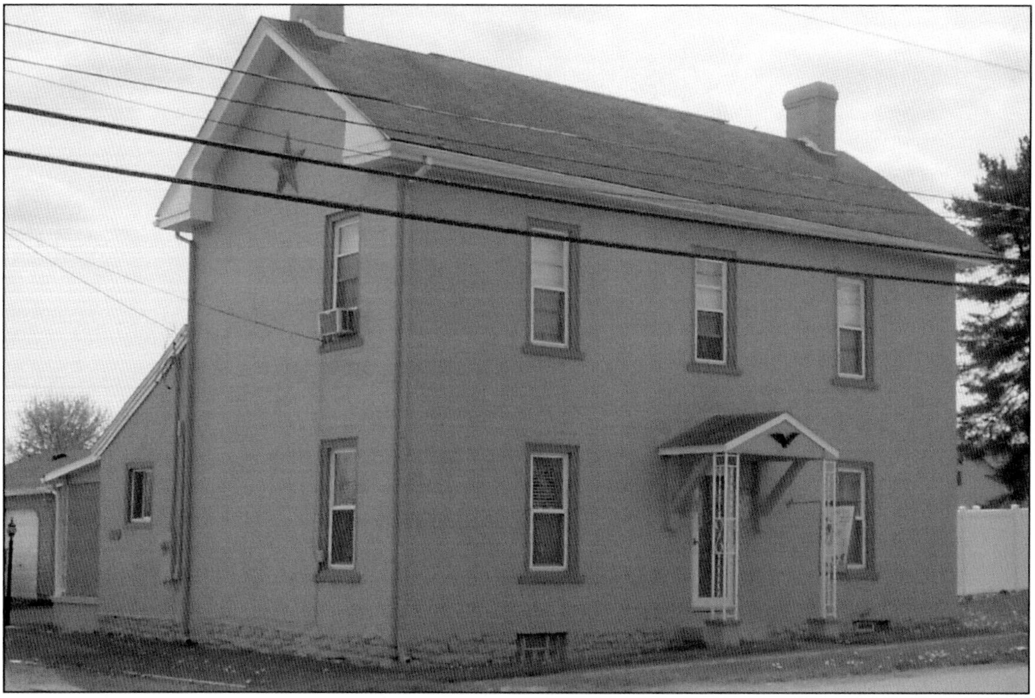

The first flour mill in town was built in 1890 by George Barclay on Pine and South Streets. Next door to the flour mill was this brick house, which is still standing today. (Courtesy of Carmichaels Area Historical Society.)

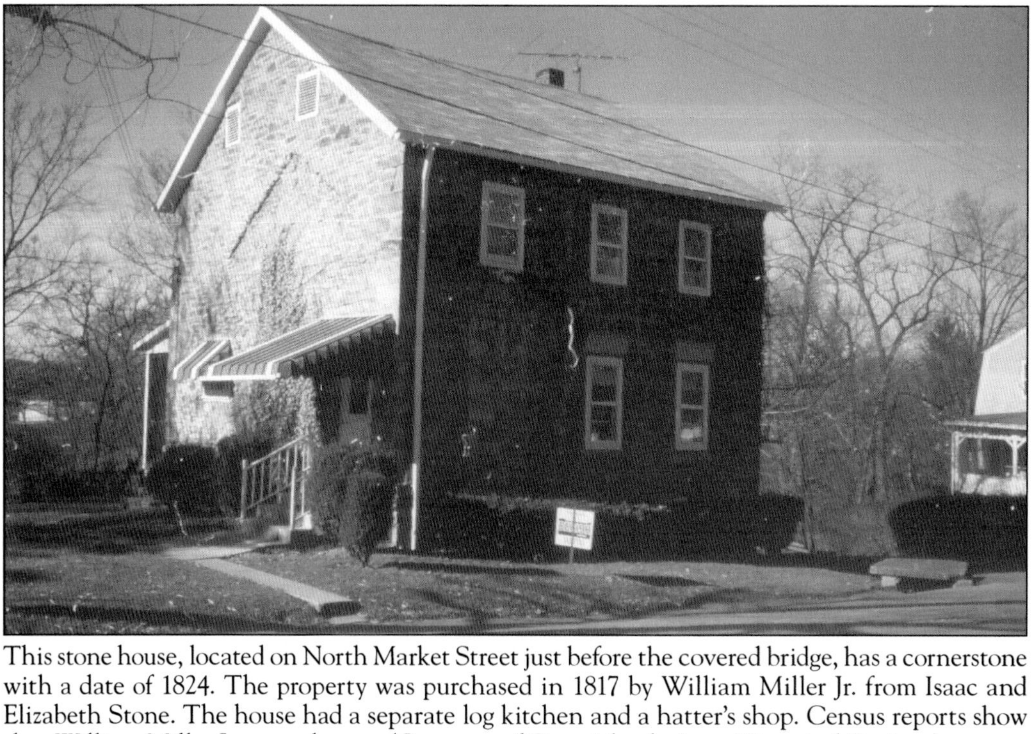

This stone house, located on North Market Street just before the covered bridge, has a cornerstone with a date of 1824. The property was purchased in 1817 by William Miller Jr. from Isaac and Elizabeth Stone. The house had a separate log kitchen and a hatter's shop. Census reports show that William Miller Jr. was a hatter. (Courtesy of Carmichaels Area Historical Society.)

Four

Schools and Churches

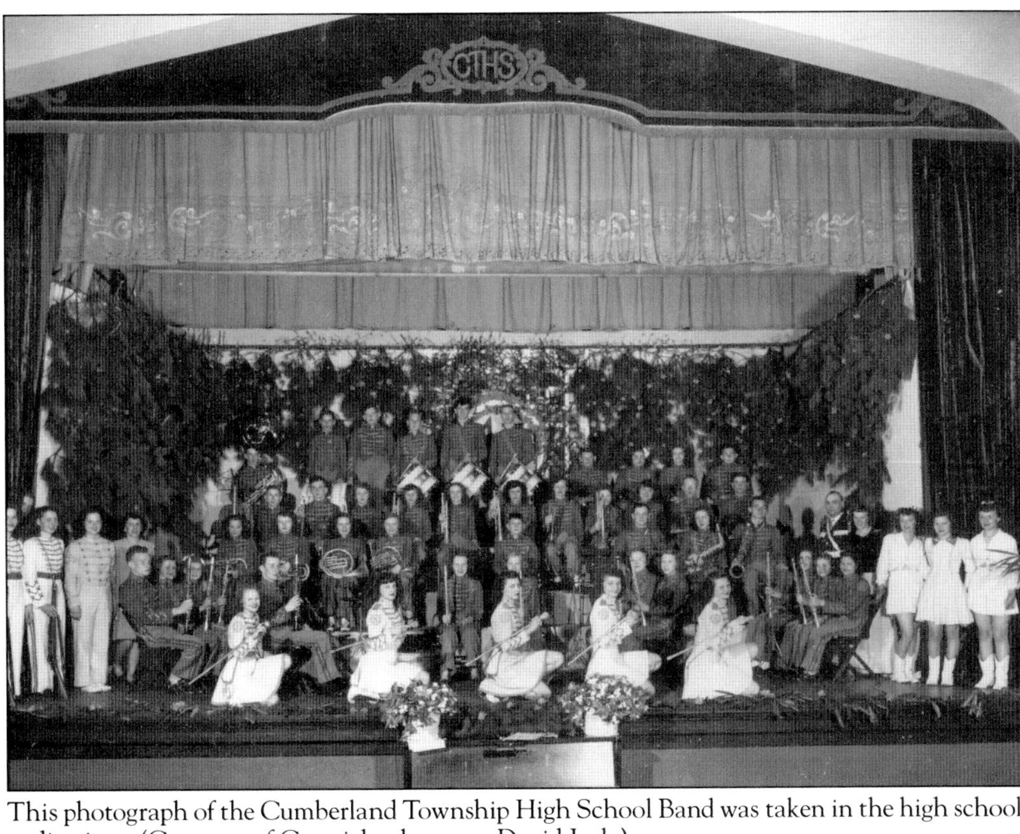

This photograph of the Cumberland Township High School Band was taken in the high school's auditorium. (Courtesy of Carmichaels mayor David Jack.)

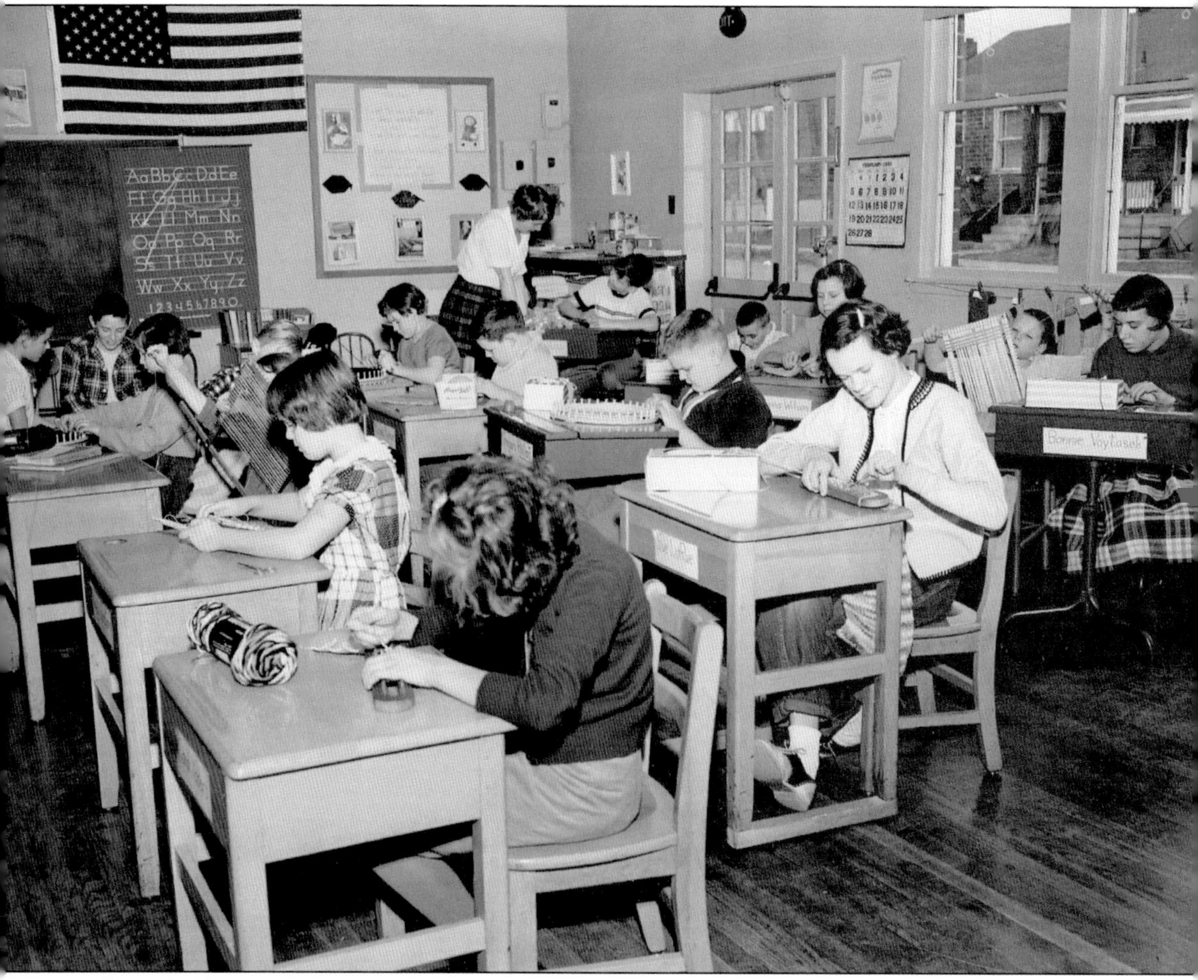

These children are participating in a special program in the kindergarten facility at Cumberland Village. A home community, Cumberland Village was built by the government during World War II to house industrial workers and returning veterans. Some of the students' names are visible on the front of their desks. (Courtesy of Flenniken Memorial Library.)

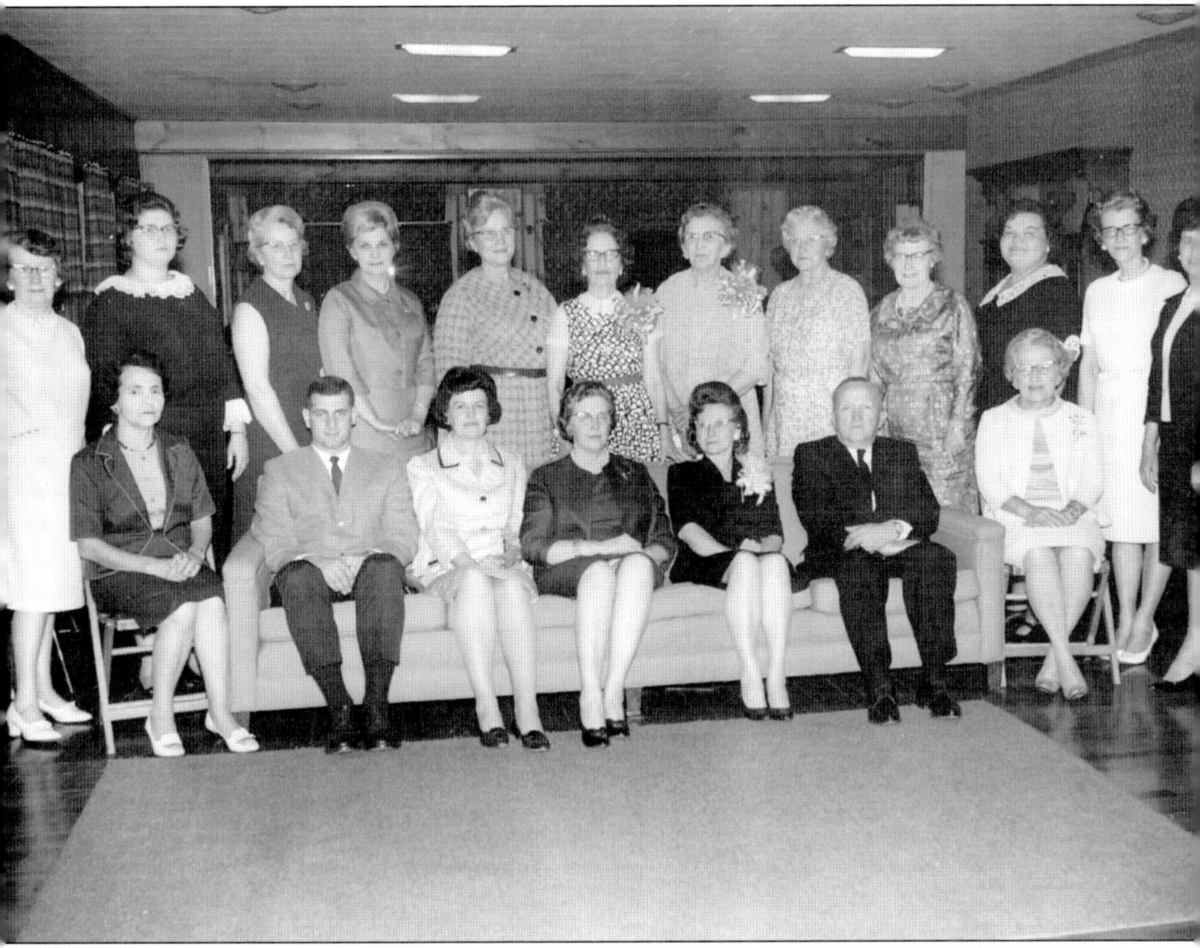

These are the teachers and principal of the Crucible Elementary School. From left to right are (sitting) Loretta Burch, Frank Rizzo, Winella Gray, Aldra Hartley, Billie Hathaway, Principal Joshua Guesman, and Martha McKee; (standing) Margaret Conner, Brenda Hartley, Hazel Reynolds, Genevieve Ross, Leora Hobbs, Margaret Baily, Ellen Gideon, Helen Hart, Opal Murphy, Dolores Zoldos, Bernice Feather, and Lucy Rumancik. Not pictured are Margaret Randolph and Ruth Kerr. (Courtesy of Carmichaels Area Historical Society.)

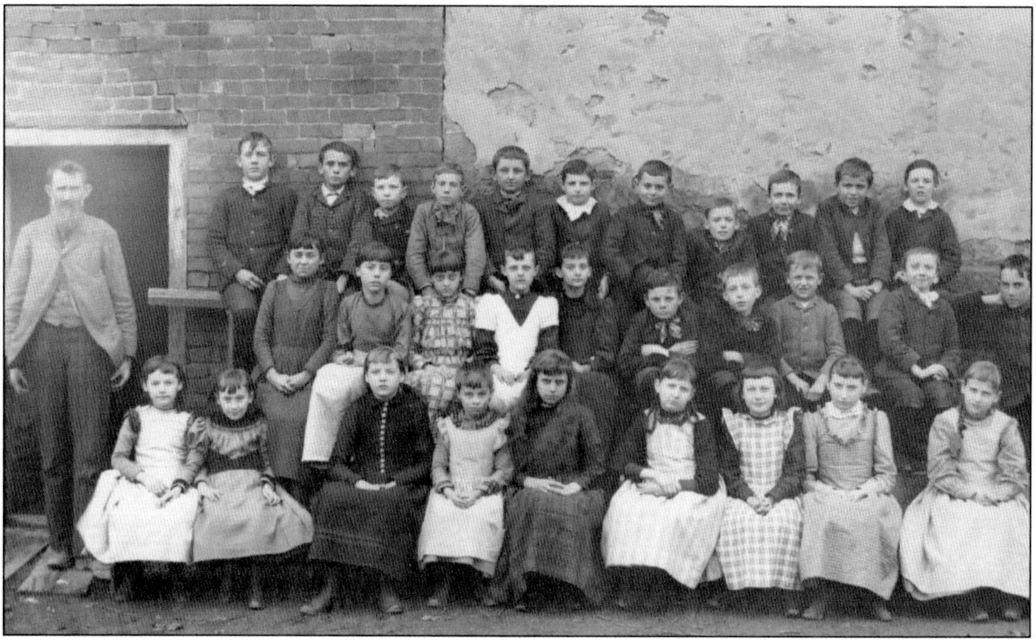

This photograph was taken outside of the Greene Academy. A few years prior to the school's closing in 1893, it served as an elementary school. At left is the teacher, Thomas Crago. The students are, from left to right, (first row) Mary Miller, Mary Laidley, Anna Gwynne, Jessie Curtis, Jessie Draden, Helen Armstrong, Sara Long, Anna Pennington, and Mary Rice; (second row) Fanny Donahoo, Ella McWilliams, Isa Burnette, Alice Curl, Lillian Davidson, Earl Miller, Clarence Patterson, Orton Clawson, Wilbur Rogers, and John Wiley; (third row) Anson Randolph, Jessie Kerr, Alfred Armstrong, James ?, James Flenniken, McClintock Hart, Joe Richey, Walter Barkman, Eddie Burnette, Jesse Kerr, and Harry Baily. (Courtesy of Greene Academy of Art.)

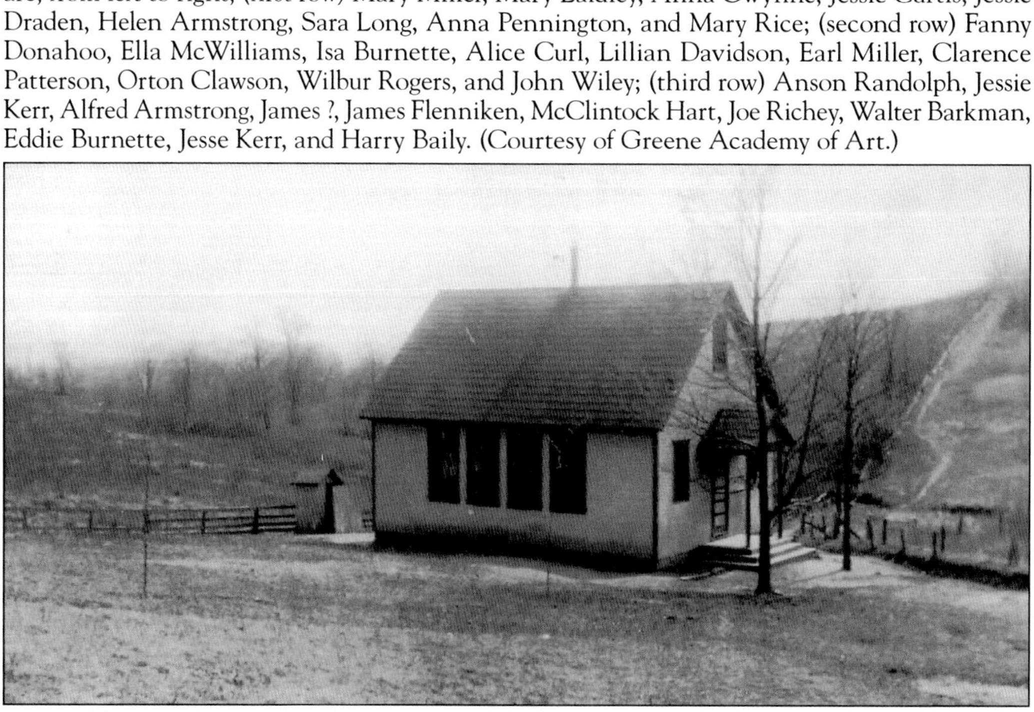

Pictured here is the Crago Schoolhouse, which was located on Carmichaels Crucible Road. At one time, the school was also known as the Oak Grove School. One of the teachers at this school was Ellen Patterson Gideon. John Menhart, a local resident, purchased the schoolhouse. (Courtesy of Susan Gideon Lawrence.)

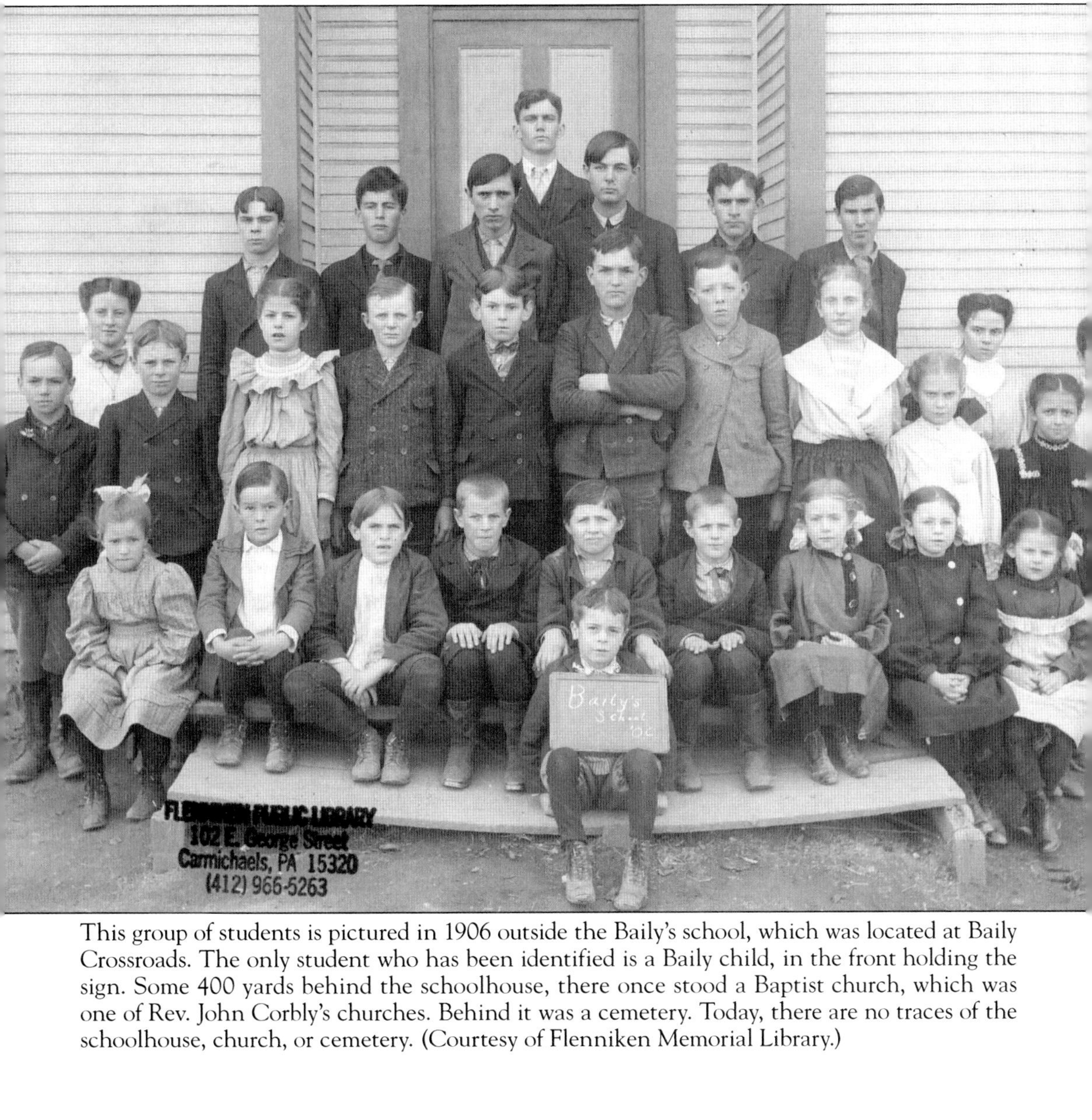

This group of students is pictured in 1906 outside the Baily's school, which was located at Baily Crossroads. The only student who has been identified is a Baily child, in the front holding the sign. Some 400 yards behind the schoolhouse, there once stood a Baptist church, which was one of Rev. John Corbly's churches. Behind it was a cemetery. Today, there are no traces of the schoolhouse, church, or cemetery. (Courtesy of Flenniken Memorial Library.)

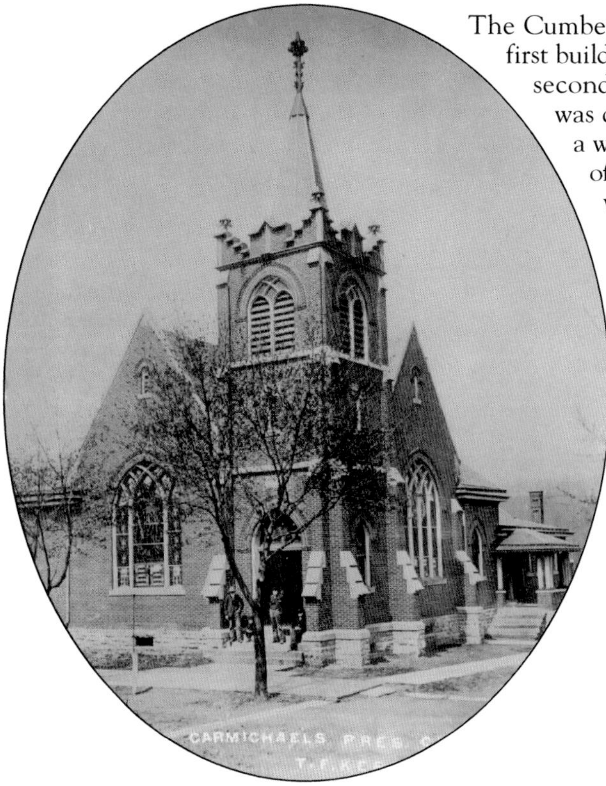

The Cumberland Presbyterian Church erected its first building in 1832 and used it until 1866. The second building erected on the present site was dedicated in 1869 but was destroyed by a wind storm in 1902, which took the roof off. The third building opened in 1905 and was destroyed by fire in 1922. A fourth building has had renovations over the years, the most recent in 2016. In 1967, five Presbyterian churches merged to form the Greene Valley Presbyterian Church. (Courtesy of Flenniken Memorial Library.)

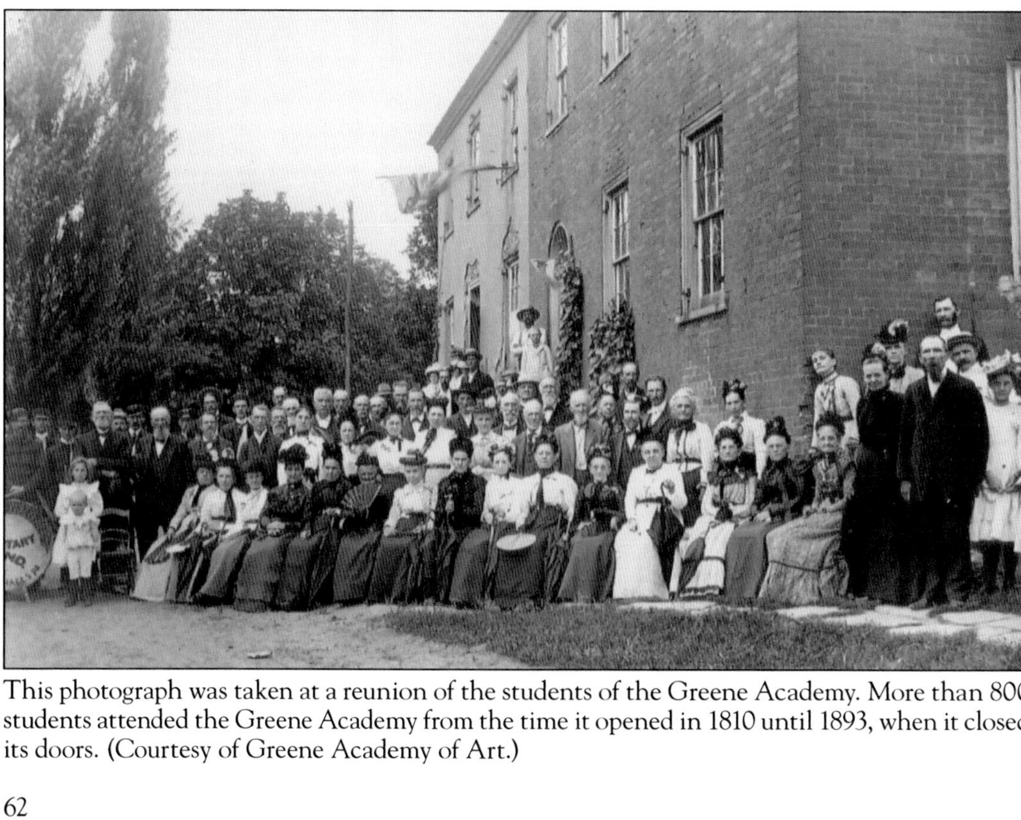

This photograph was taken at a reunion of the students of the Greene Academy. More than 800 students attended the Greene Academy from the time it opened in 1810 until 1893, when it closed its doors. (Courtesy of Greene Academy of Art.)

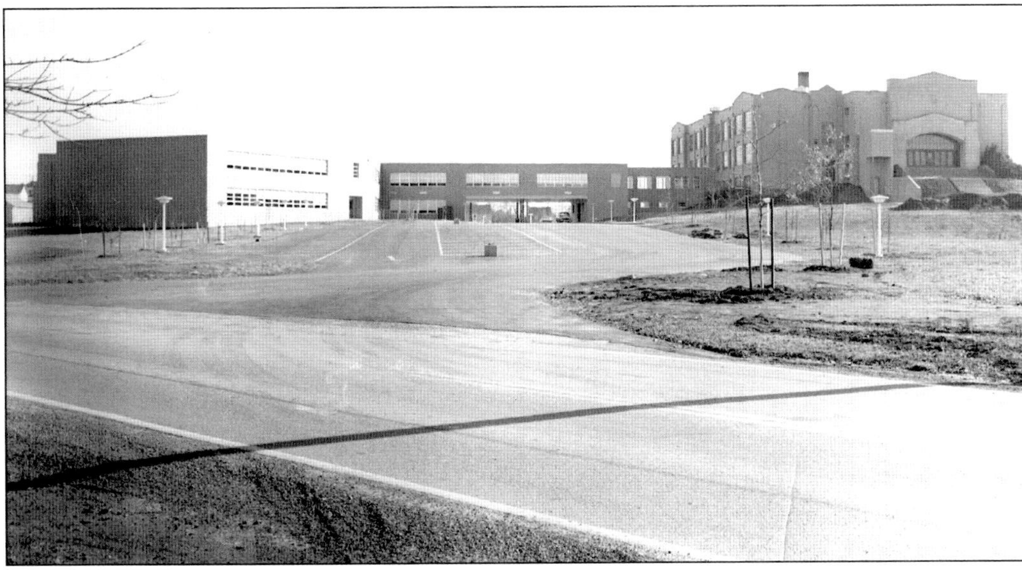

The school district broke ground in 1928 on a portion of the former J.W. Hathaway property. The original three-story brick building was completed in 1929, allowing the graduating class of 1929 to hold commencement in the newly constructed auditorium. In 1967, an addition was made to the building. The three-story side was used as the junior high school, and the new two-story addition was used as the senior high. The school has seen recent renovations creating a new entrance and additional classrooms. (Courtesy of Flenniken Memorial Library.)

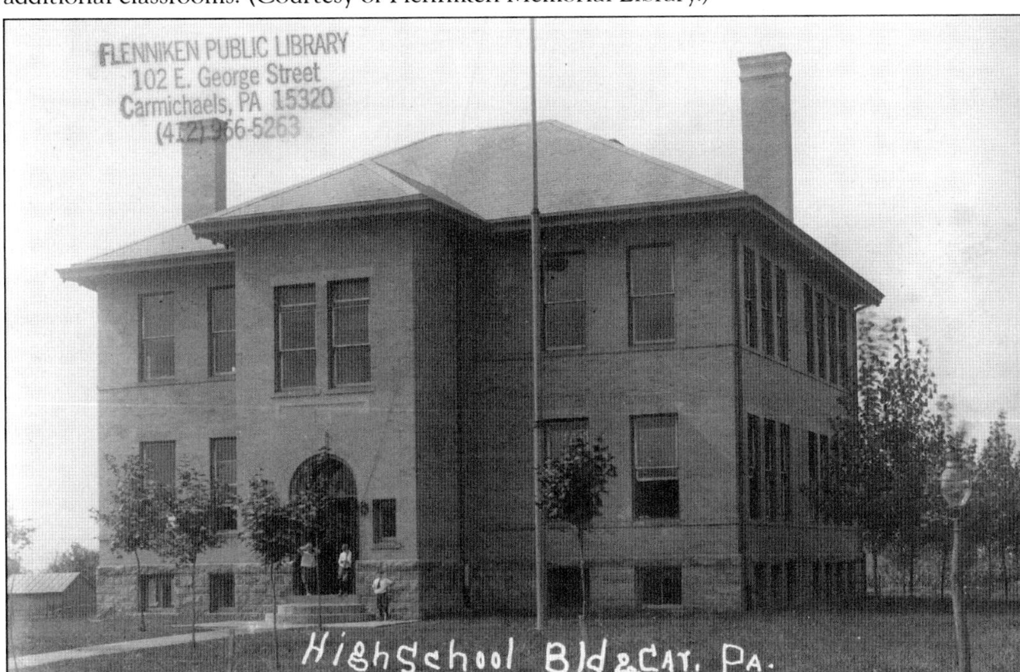

The Cumberland Township High School, built in 1910, was located on South Market Street. The brick building had three classrooms, an office, and an auditorium. Around 1919, a chemistry lab was added in the basement. Around 1923, due to continuous growth, the auditorium was converted to classrooms. (Courtesy of Flenniken Memorial Library.)

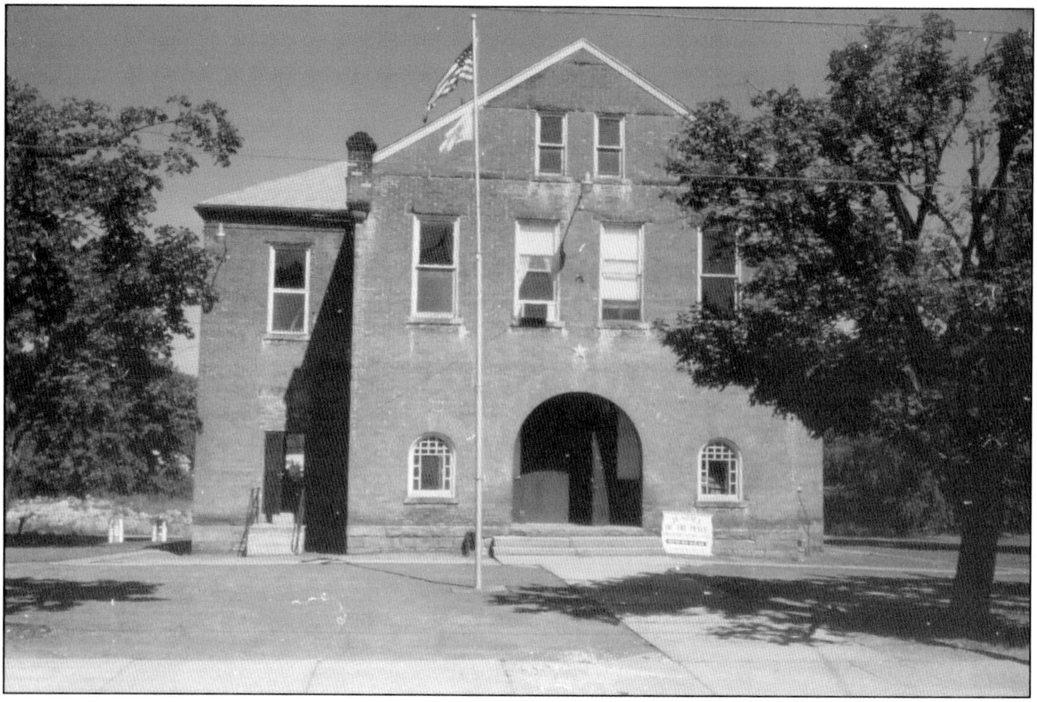

In 1893, the Carmichaels Borough School was built on Greene Street next to the First Presbyterian Church. The building had two floors, with the first- through fourth-grade classes on the first floor and the fifth- through eighth-grade classes on the second floor. After the elementary schools in the township merged, the Borough School was closed. It was then used as a municipal building by the Carmichaels Borough until it was badly burned in 1978. (Courtesy of Flenniken Memorial Library.)

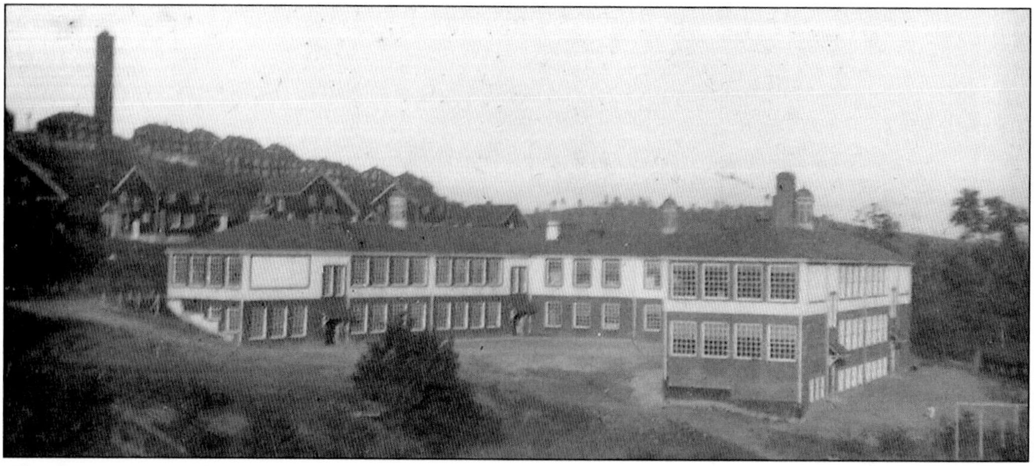

The first section of the Nemacolin Elementary School was completed and opened in the fall of the 1919–1920 school year. This first section was constructed of brick and had eight rooms. In August 1924, an addition to the building was completed. Robert A. Korcheck, Nemacolin resident and historian, recorded that, by 1934, the Nemacolin Elementary School had an enrollment of approximately 900 students, many bussed from the Carmichaels area. (Courtesy of Brice and Linda Rush and the Robert Korcheck collection.)

This is the school bell used for the Carmichaels Borough School from 1893 until 1966. Former students recalled that the bell hung in the belfry, and was rung by each student taking their turn standing on the landing and pulling the rope to ring it. The bell was so large that a small child, pulling hard on the rope to make it ring, would be picked up into the air as the bell swung back and forth. The bell, which is on permanent display, was donated to the Greene Academy of Art in 2008 by the Carmichaels Borough School Reunion Committee. (Courtesy of Greene Academy of Art.)

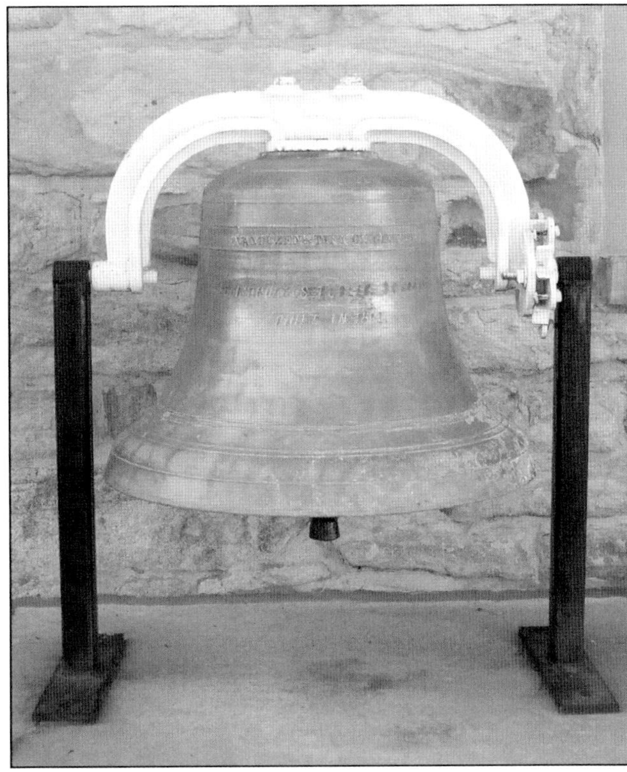

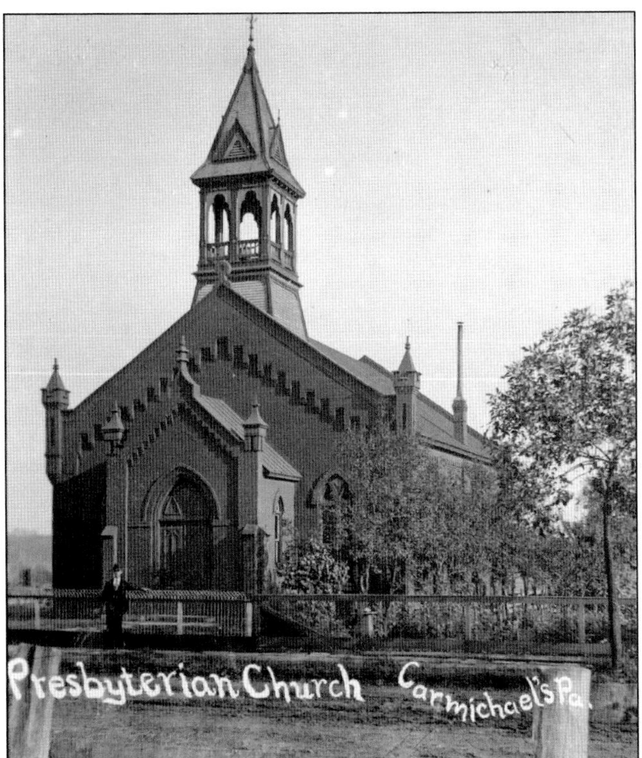

The New Providence Presbyterian Church began in the late 1700s with a three-room log structure in the location known as "the Glades," which became the nickname of the church. Since that time, three other buildings were erected for the Glades Church, known also as "the country church." Another building was erected in town to accommodate those living in town and along Muddy Creek. This photograph shows the beauty of the New Providence Presbyterian Church, known as the "in-town" church, located on East George Street, built in 1852 and used until the 1920s. It was later the home of the American Legion Post No. 400; currently, it is vacant. (Courtesy of Brice and Linda Rush.)

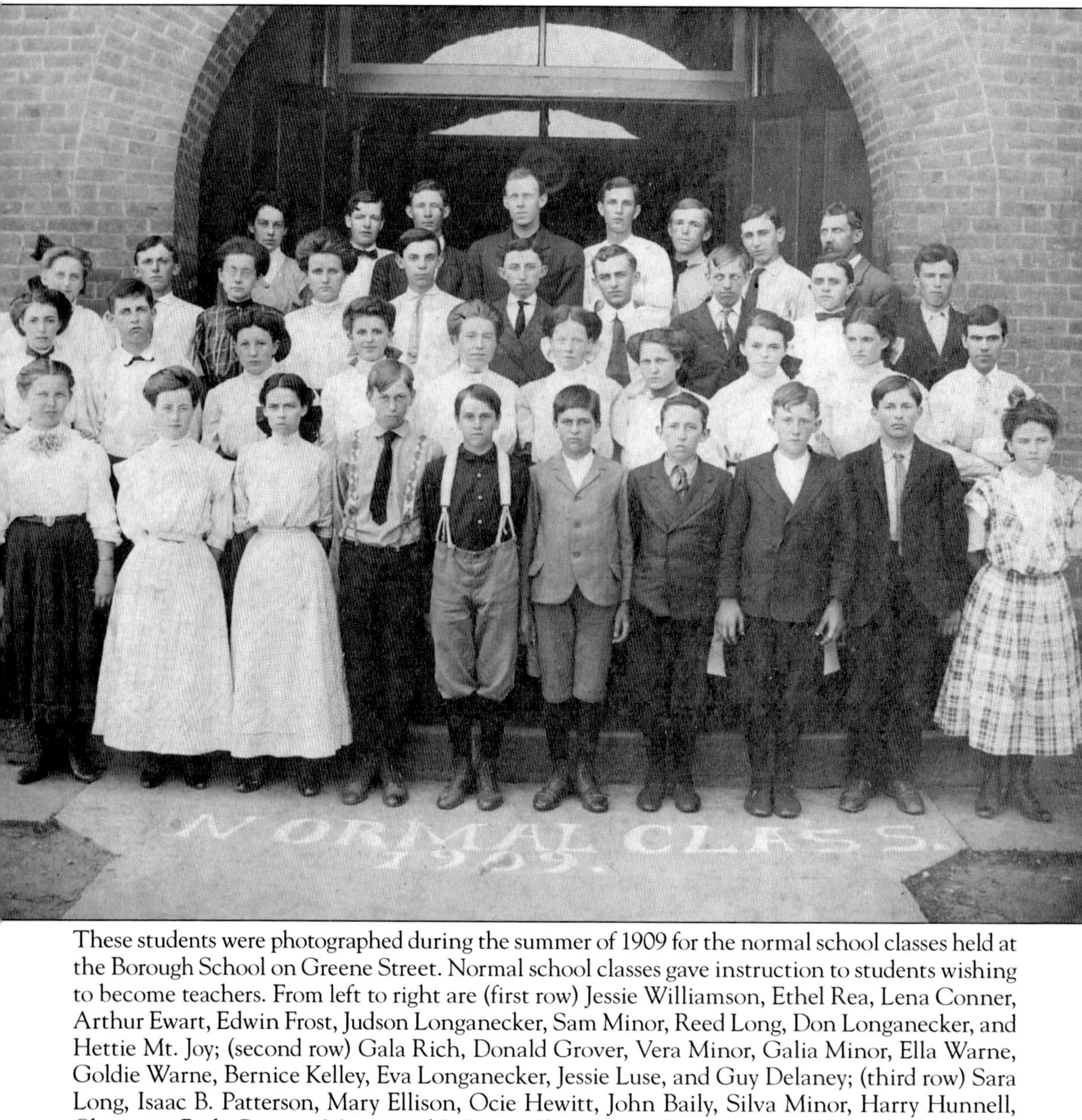

These students were photographed during the summer of 1909 for the normal school classes held at the Borough School on Greene Street. Normal school classes gave instruction to students wishing to become teachers. From left to right are (first row) Jessie Williamson, Ethel Rea, Lena Conner, Arthur Ewart, Edwin Frost, Judson Longanecker, Sam Minor, Reed Long, Don Longanecker, and Hettie Mt. Joy; (second row) Gala Rich, Donald Grover, Vera Minor, Galia Minor, Ella Warne, Goldie Warne, Bernice Kelley, Eva Longanecker, Jessie Luse, and Guy Delaney; (third row) Sara Long, Isaac B. Patterson, Mary Ellison, Ocie Hewitt, John Baily, Silva Minor, Harry Hunnell, Chauncey Rich, Pearson Minor, and J. Stone; (fourth row) Maggie Hart, Walter Huggins, Levi Fuller, Cecil Morris, Benjamin Crago, Arthur Titus, Ross Long, and Professor Williamson. (Courtesy of Bill Groves.)

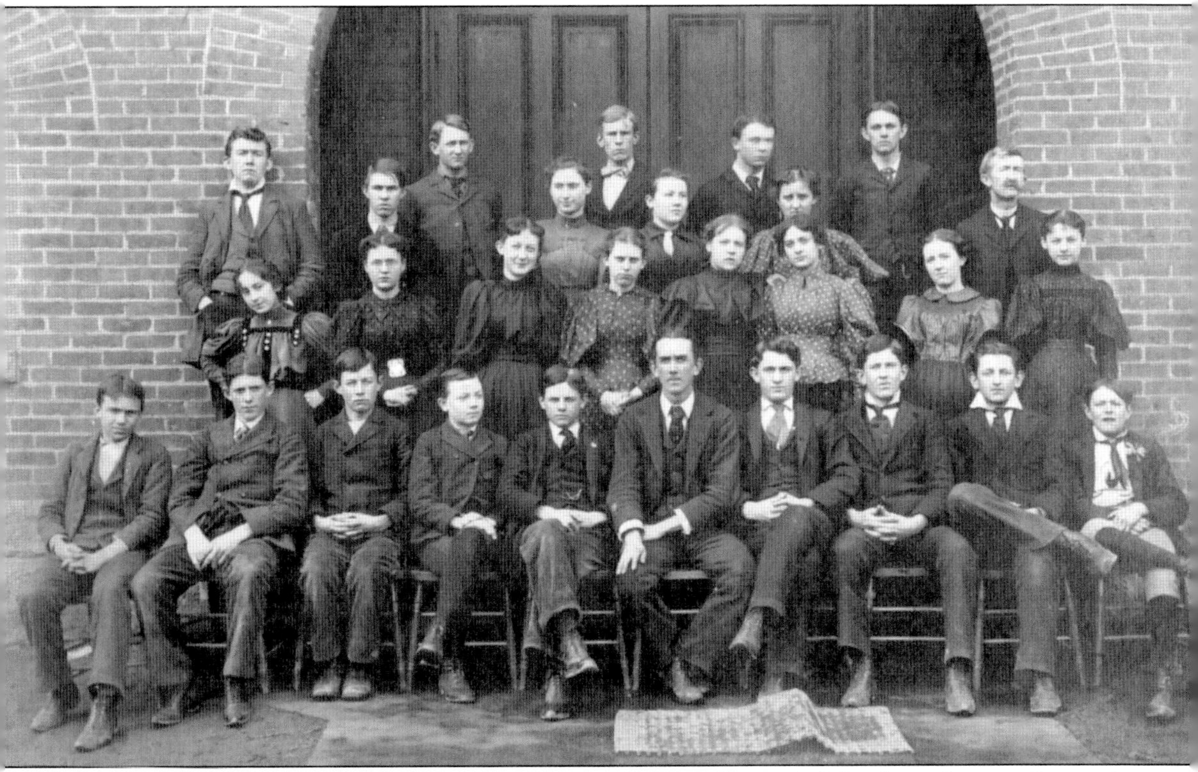

The date of this photograph of students at the Carmichaels Borough School is unknown. Pictured are, from left to right, (first row) Jesse Kerr, Ray Evans, Earl Smith, Wilbur Rogers, Earl Miller, John W. Wiley, Anson Randolph, Robert Hathaway, McClintock Hart, and Walter Barkman; (second row) Mamie Laidley, Lida Kerr, Sara Long, Jessie Drayden, Anna Gwynne, Lillian Davidson, Helen Armstrong, and Mary Miller; (third row) Ed Wiley, Linta Sharpnack, Anna Pennington, Thelma Rogers, Eta Barclay, and teacher George Davis; (fourth row) Frank Patterson, Fred Flenniken, Ellis Hawkins, and Alex Davidson. (Courtesy of Bill Groves.)

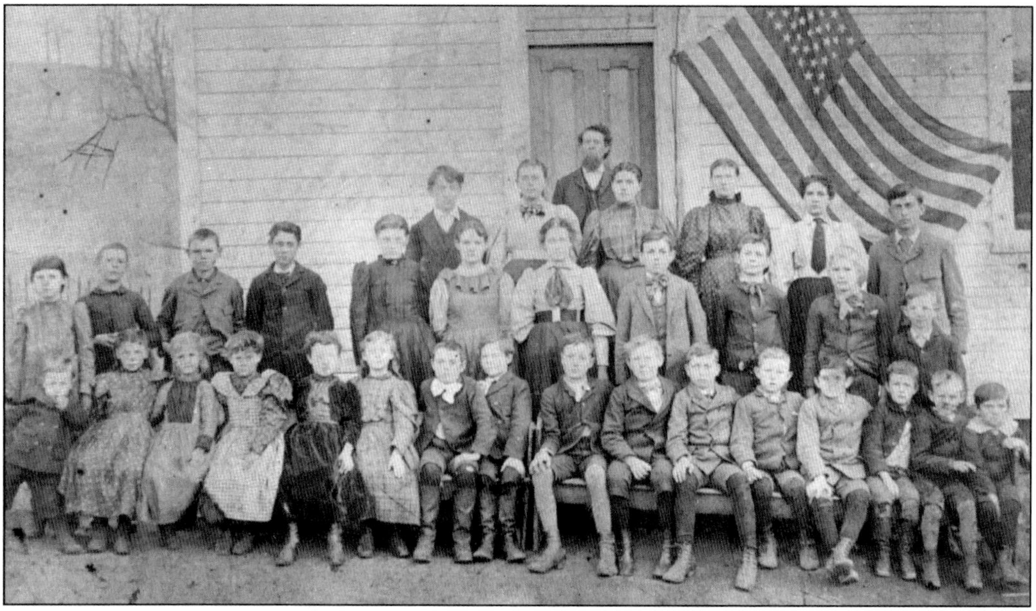

This picture of Hart's School in Pierceville, now known as Ceylon, was taken in 1896. From left to right are (first row) Bill Ullery, Ethel Cummins, Ida Stone, Alice Ullery, Goldie Stewart, Loma Stephenson, Bert Ireland, Hugh Hartley, Charles Stewart, Clayton Hartley, Chester Crumrine, Earl Christopher, Earl Baily, Jimmy Stone, Frances Christopher, and Frank Baily; (second row) Kate Ullery, Minor Stone, Harry Ullery, Charles Cunningham, Kate Hohn, Mary Stewart, Ethel Stephenson, Jonah Hart, Jess Hart, Francis Craig, and Orval Christopher; (third row) Frank Crumrine, Eva Hartley, Bessie Stephenson, Ida Mundell, Flo Stephenson, and Walter Crumrine. In the doorway is the teacher, Dode Hartley. (Courtesy of Brice and Linda Rush.)

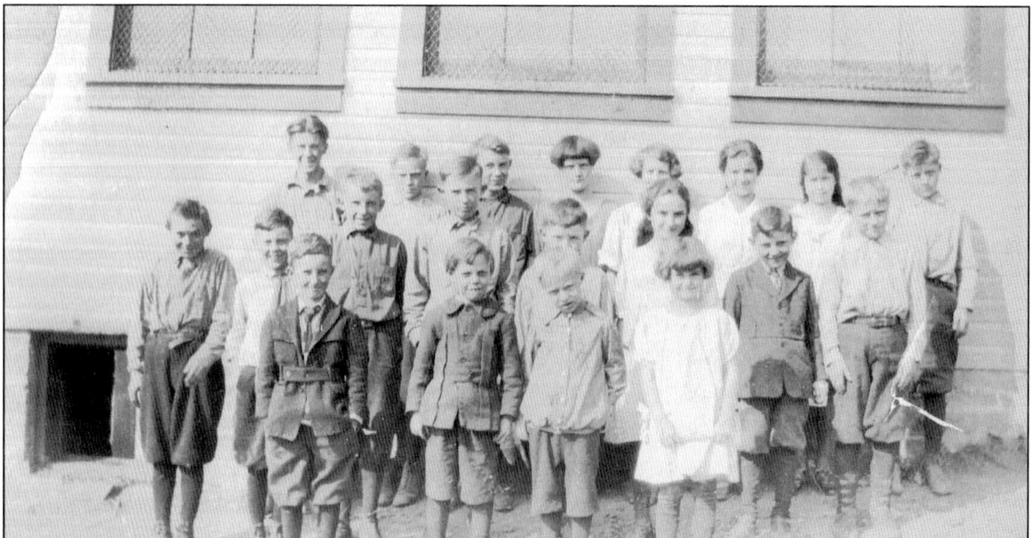

This is a group of Crago School students. This school was on Crucible Road and was also known as the Oak Grove School. The only student identified is Leora McCann Haver, who is pictured in the back row second from the right. (Courtesy of Dorothy Cole.)

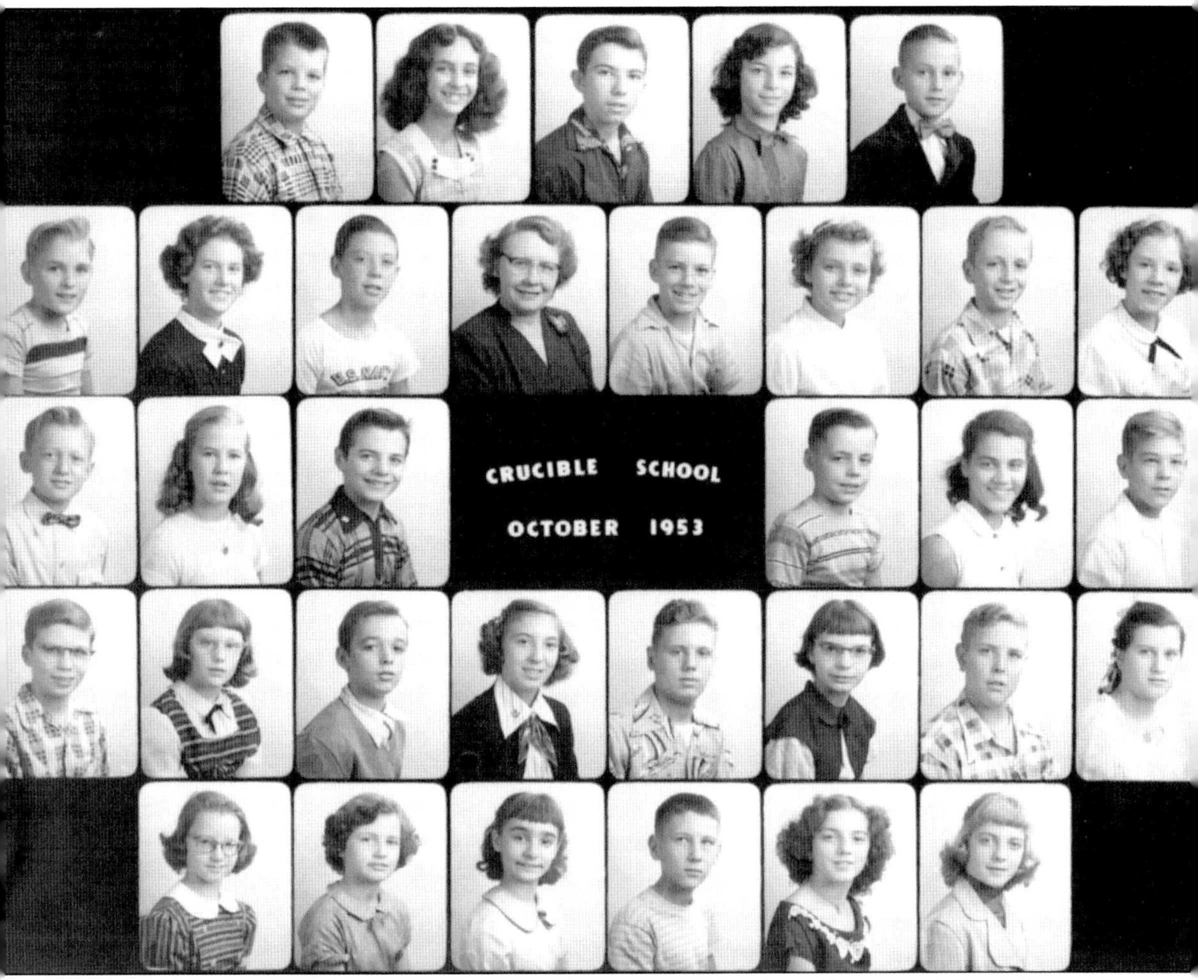

Pictured here in October 1953 are sixth-grade students of the Crucible Grade School. From left to right are (top row) Charles Tillson, Lynette Crow, Steve Blumish, Judith Rockwell, and George Poling; (second row) Charles Douglas, Jane Dorricott, Earl Ketchum, teacher Mrs. Murphy, James Hixon, Doris Yakubec, Daniel Novak, and Anna Stasko; (third row) Robert Hlubin, Elaine Huntley, Joseph Burvan, Forrest Solomon, Joanne Cardilla, and Terry Austin; (fourth row) George Medunick, Carol Waters, Joseph O'Laughlin, Marlene Kronk, Sherman Davidson, Rita Savanik, Charles Buskirk, and Nancy Novak; (bottom row) Susan Discutner, Billie Jo Bair, D.L.M., Edward Wiggins, Josephine Lugosavich, and Judith Danforth. Not pictured is Jacqueline Mahle. (Courtesy of Donna Milak Rathburn.)

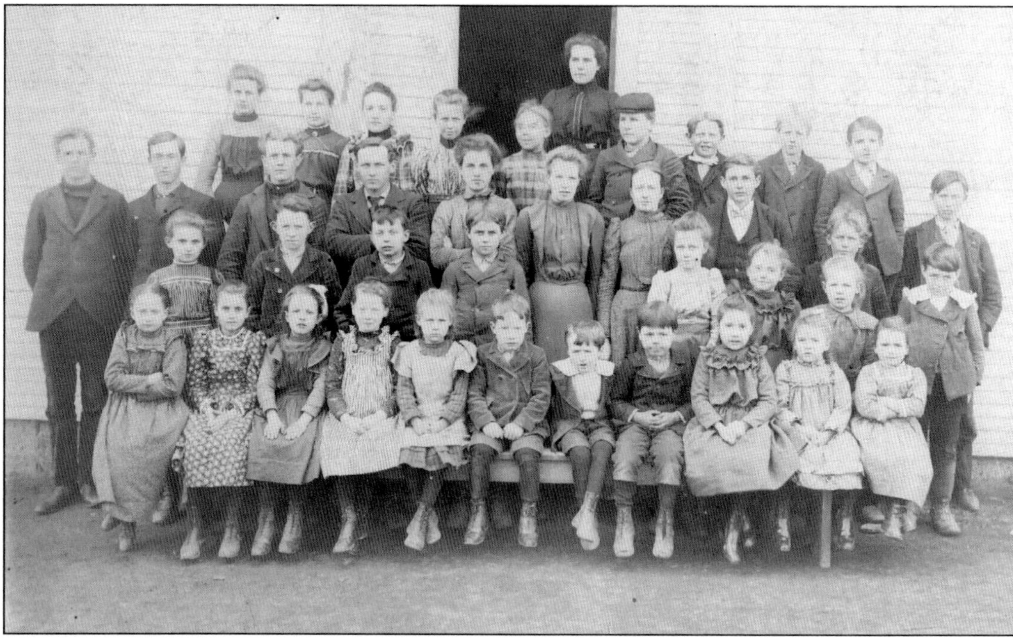

From the 1800s and into the early to mid-1900s, there were numerous one-room schoolhouses, and a few with two rooms, within Cumberland Township and Carmichaels. Among those schools were Baily's, Rea's, Conner's, Neels, Crago, Barnes, Houston's, Hart's, Black's, Long's, Donley's, Wiley Height's, Khedive, Fairdale, Strawn, Center, Live Easy, and several more. Education of the children was very important to the settlers of this area. (Courtesy of Flenniken Memorial Library.)

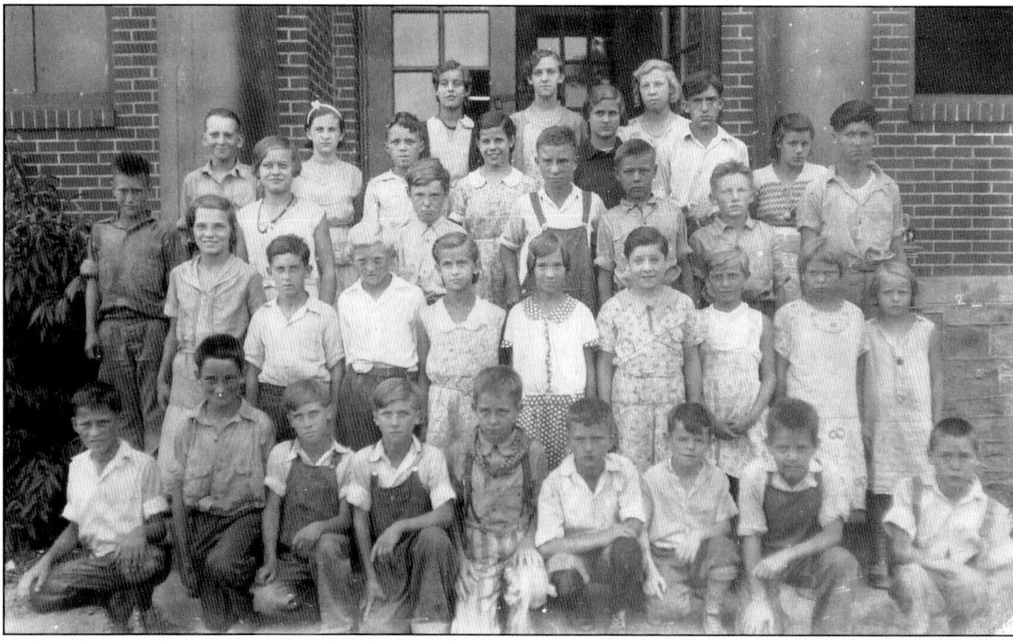

Taken during the 1932–1933 school year, this photograph shows students at the Conner's School on Route 88. One of the teachers who taught at this school was Lon R. McMinn. The only child identified in this photograph is Edward McMinn, pictured in the first row, second from left. (Courtesy of Marcine Helmick McMinn.)

Five

Around the Township

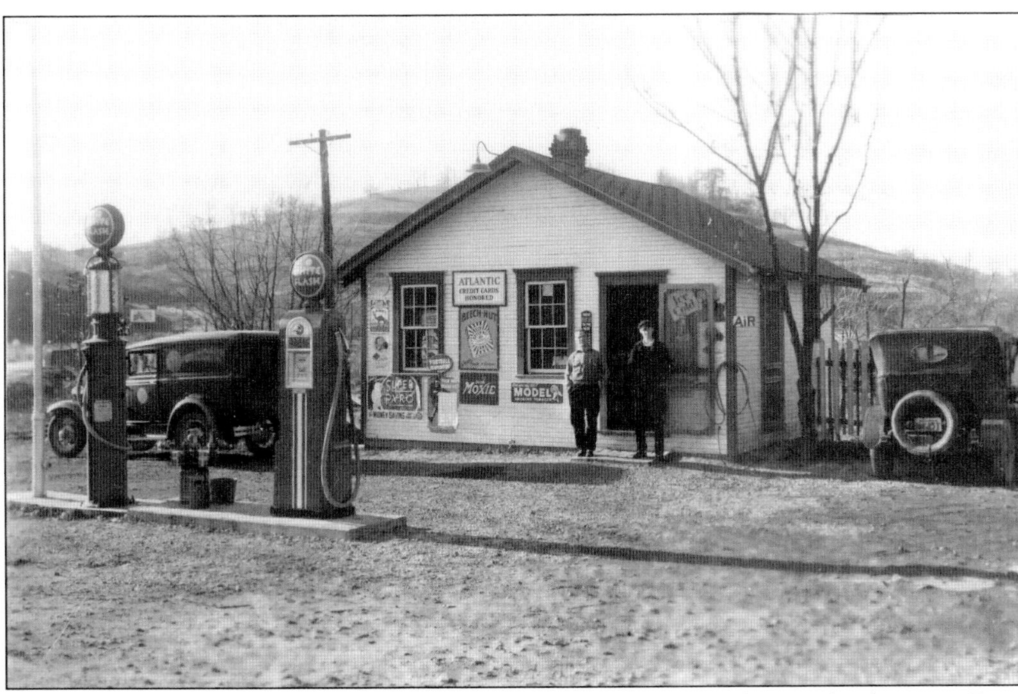

Grooms's Hilltop Service Station, operated by Raymond W. Grooms of Carmichaels, was on Route 88 North, just past the Carmichaels Golf Course on the top of the hill. (Courtesy of Greene County Historical Society and Museum.)

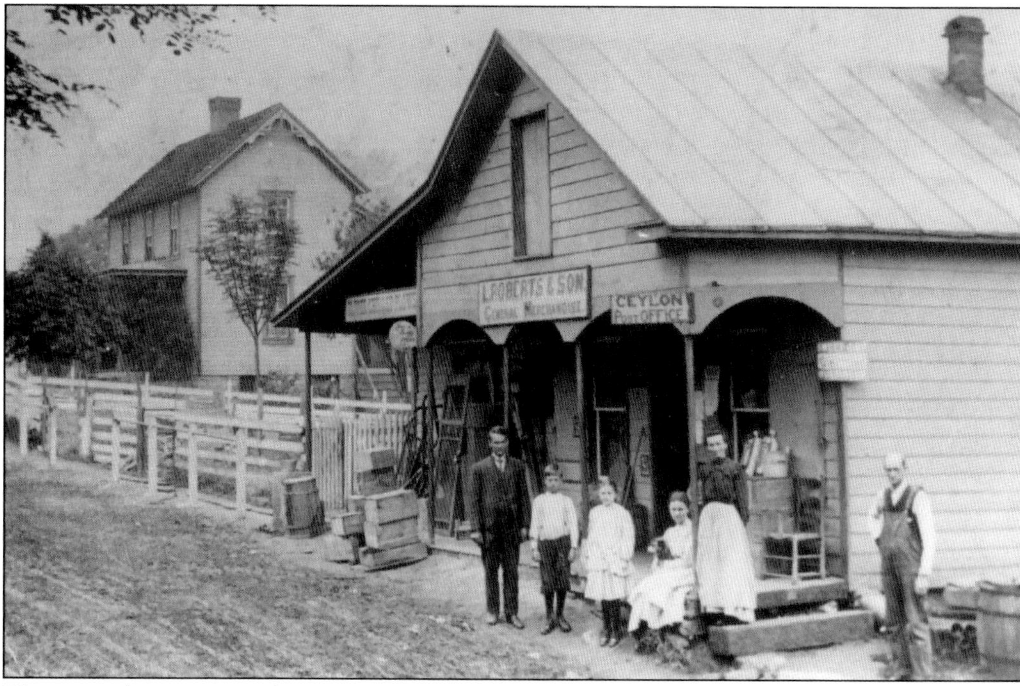

The general store in Ceylon was operated by Lemuel Roberts and his family. A post office was established in Ceylon in 1868, and William Lindsey was its first postmaster. Records show there were six postmasters. Lemuel Roberts became the postmaster on December 26, 1876, and served until May 8, 1879. The post office closed in 1917. Pictured here are, from left to right, Edward Mundell, Clyde Mundell, Emma Mary Roberts, Elsie Hartley, Clementine Robert, and Lemuel Roberts. (Courtesy of Brice and Linda Rush.)

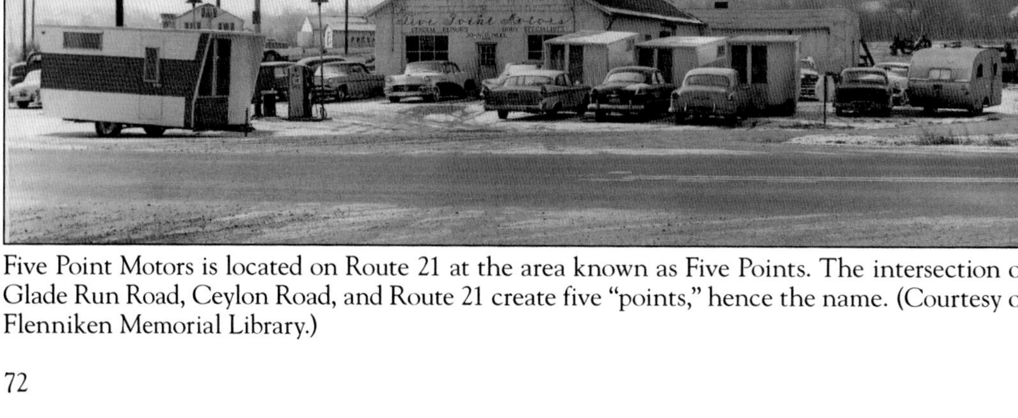

Five Point Motors is located on Route 21 at the area known as Five Points. The intersection of Glade Run Road, Ceylon Road, and Route 21 create five "points," hence the name. (Courtesy of Flenniken Memorial Library.)

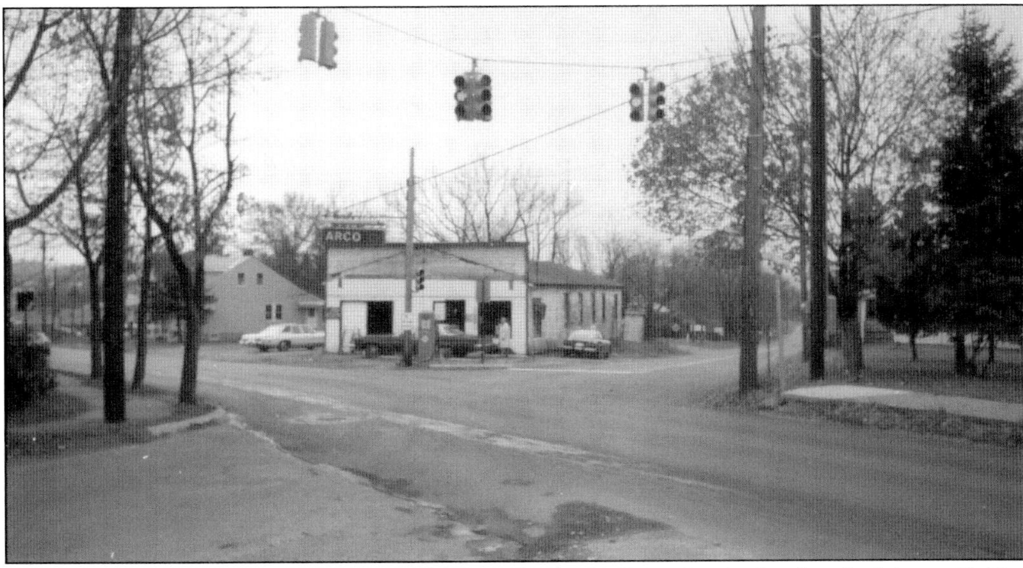

In 1922, John Zoldos, his son Steve Zoldos, and John Milnarcik, the husband of Anna Zoldos, operated a service station at the point of Route 88 and Ceylon Road. During World War II, with car business almost nonexistent, they opened a grocery store. Steve Zoldos always loved cars, and in 1952, he purchased a Tucker car agency. (Courtesy of Flenniken Memorial Library.)

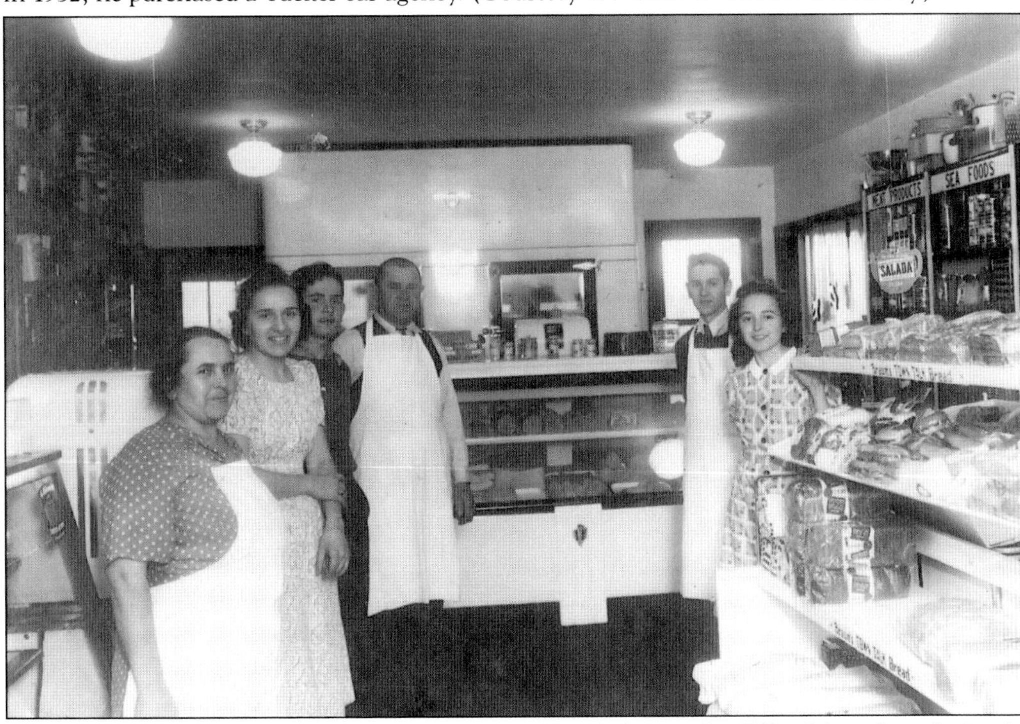

Pictured inside Sertich's store on Route 88 are, from left to right, Effie, Mary, Joseph, Joe Jr., Anthony, and Josephine. In 1938, Joseph Sertich Sr. purchased land from the Baily farm on Route 88 in the Fairdale area and built his store in 1941. Joseph was a butcher and had a slaughter permit from the state, and behind the store was a building used for slaughtering and dressing fresh meat. Joseph Sr. operated the store until 1957. (Courtesy of Stella Sertich.)

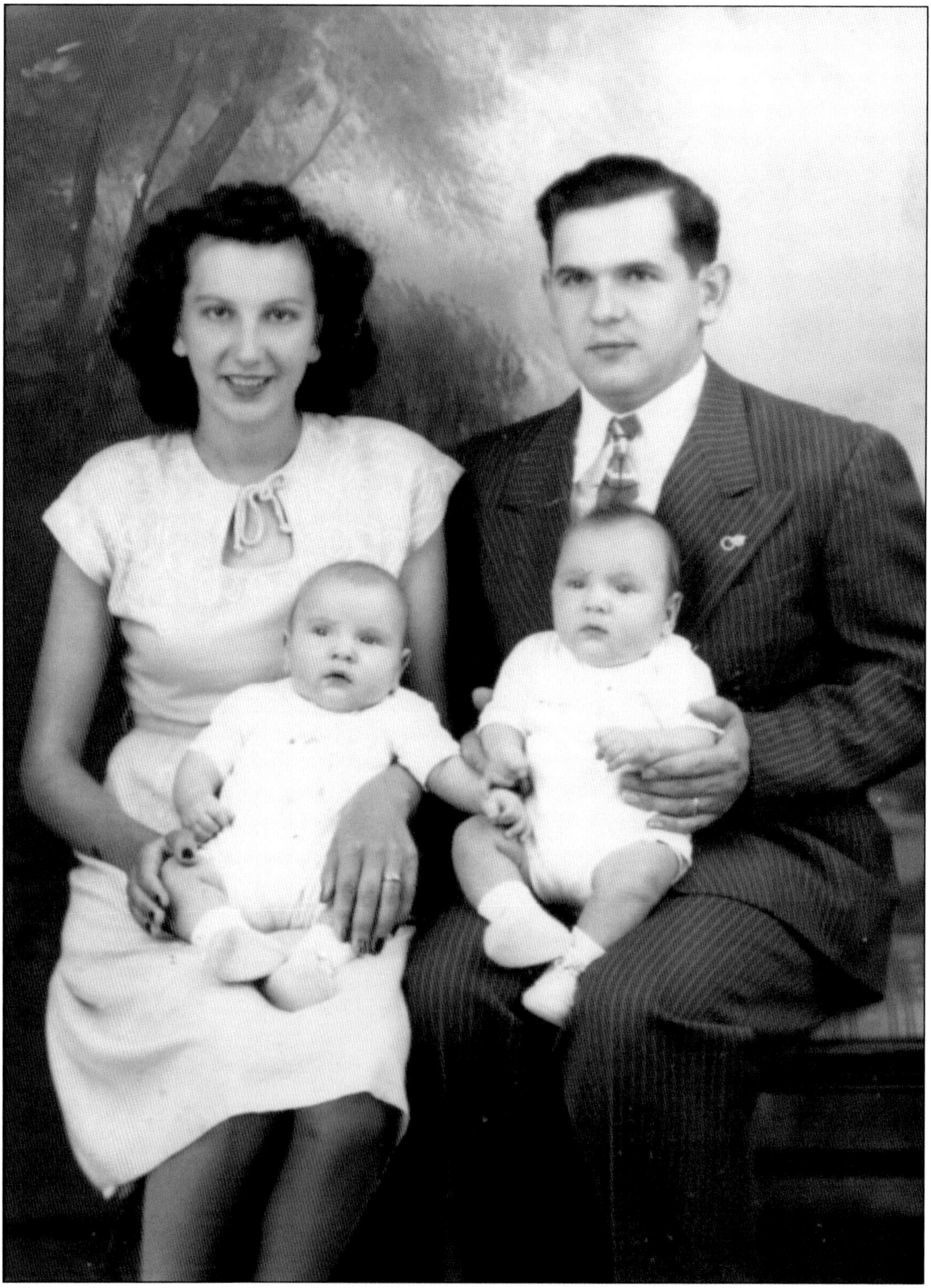

This is a lovely photograph of Joseph Sertich Jr.; his wife, Stella; and their twin sons, Joseph and John. Joseph Jr. and his wife took over the operation of Sertich's store in 1957 and ran it until 1967. The Sertich family helped local families who fell on hard times by allowing them to purchase food on credit and pay their bills a little at a time. (Courtesy of Stella Sertich.)

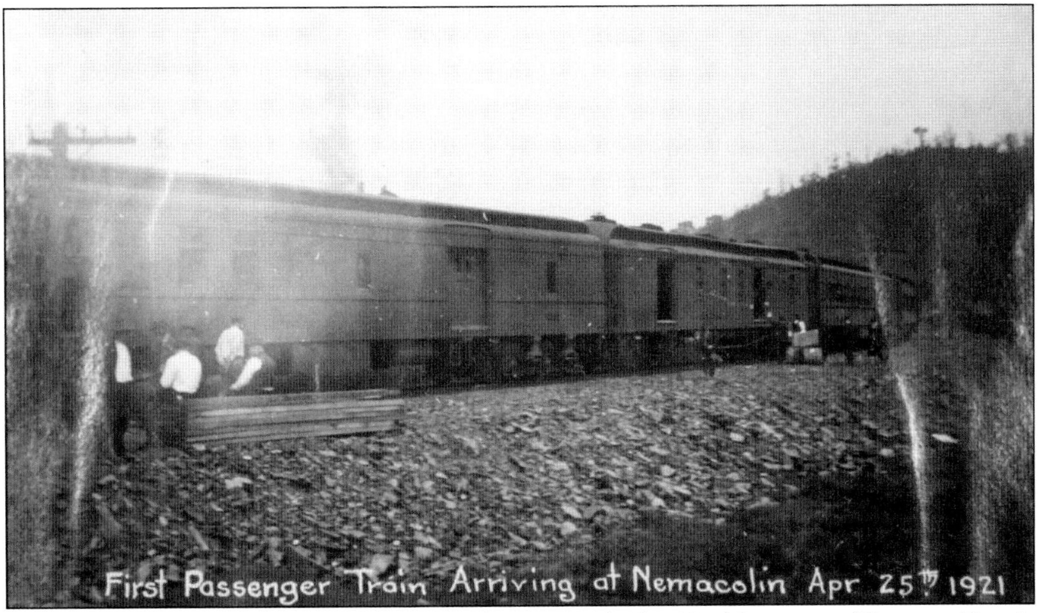

The first passenger train arrived in Nemacolin on April 25, 1921. (Courtesy of Brice and Linda Rush and the Robert Korcheck collection.)

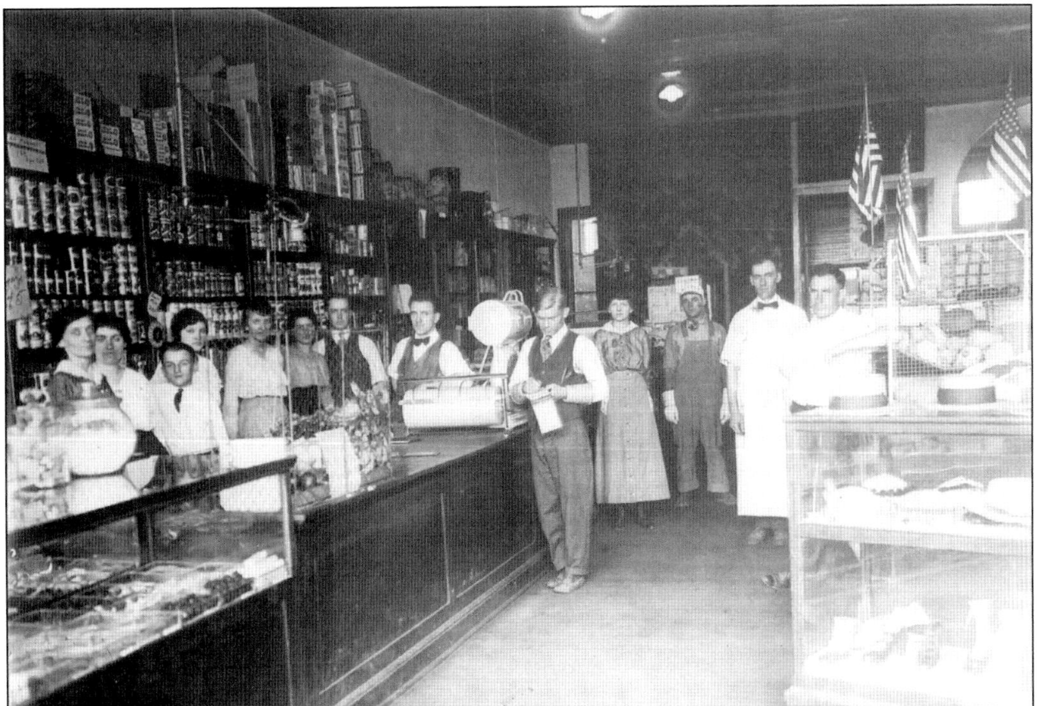
This is the interior of the Cumberland Supply Company in Crucible. Pictured are, from left to right, Lillian Davidson, Edna Gwynne Johnson, Johnny Havanis, Pearl Dayton, Ellen Patterson Gideon, Mary Mt. Joy Areford Hart, J. Vernon Moredock, ? Newcomer, Mike Urbany, Mabel Patterson Stockfish, Harry Rafter, Frank Ross, and John Areford. (Courtesy of Barbara Aspey.)

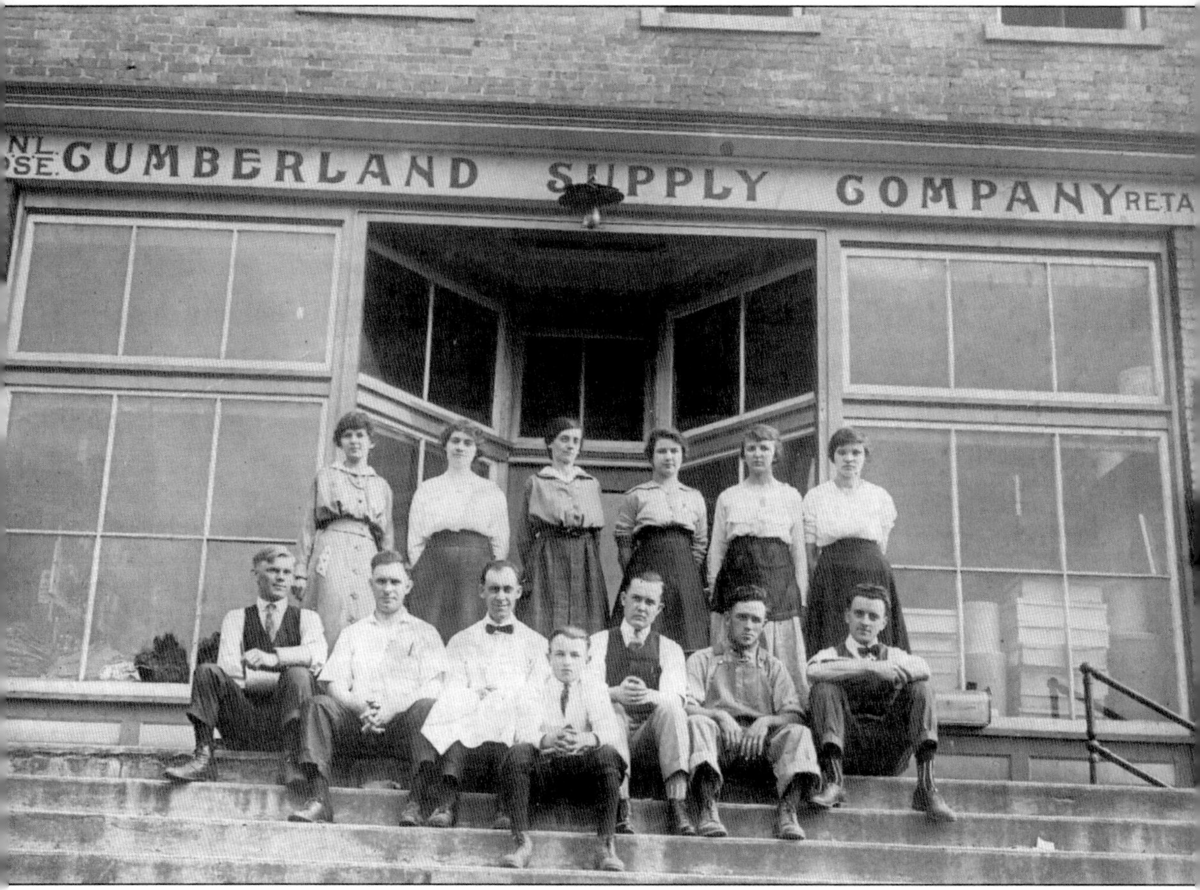

Pictured here on the steps of the Cumberland Supply Company in Crucible are, from left to right, (sitting) Mike Urbany, John Areford, Frank Ross, Johnny Havanis, J. Vernon Moredock, Harry Rafter, and ? Newcomer; (standing) Mabel Patterson Stockfish, Edna Gwynne Johnson, Lillian Davidson, Mary Mt. Joy Areford Hart, Ellen Patterson Gideon, and Pearl Dayton. (Courtesy of Barbara Aspey.)

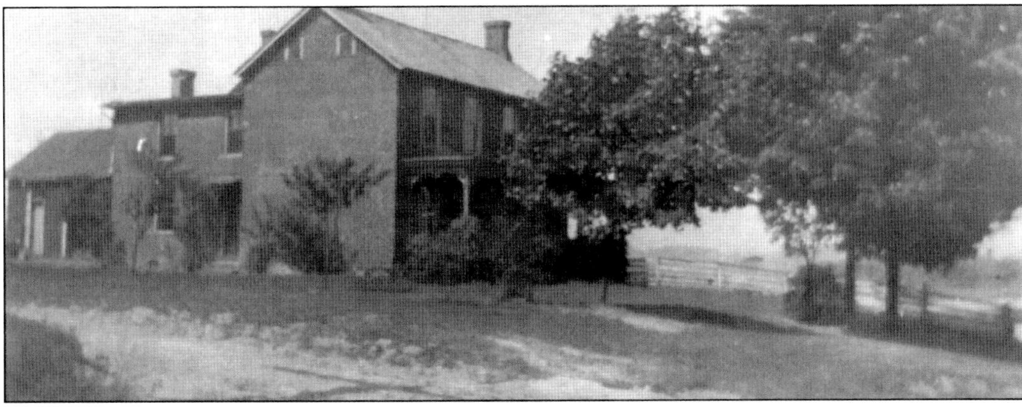

The John G. Baily farmhouse fronted on Route 88 about a quarter mile north of Carmichaels. This photograph was taken in 1909. John G. Baily was a successful dairy farmer and had a retail delivery route in Carmichaels, Dry Tavern, Fairdale, Nemacolin, Ceylon, Paisley, Live Easy, and other areas in the township. He delivered milk house-to-house, and during World War II, his cows produced more milk than any other farm in Greene County. The home, barn, and farm no longer exist. (Courtesy of Farrah Doman and the Helen Kamenos Trevorrow collection.)

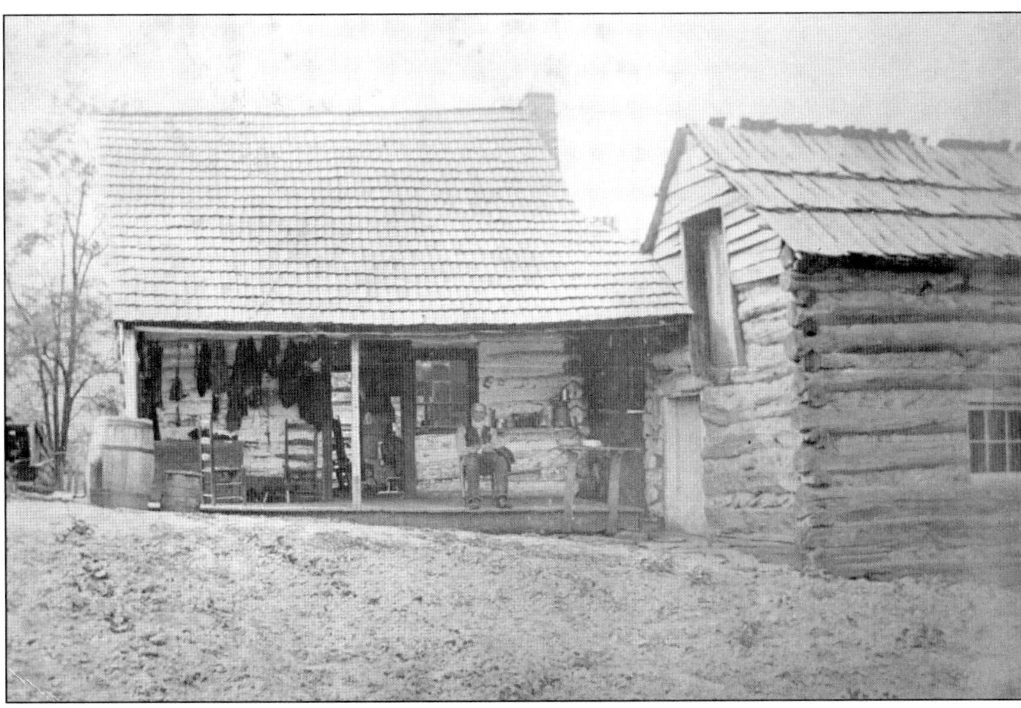

No longer in existence, this log home was once located in Ceylon, which was first named Waterford and then changed to Pierceville. (Courtesy of Flenniken Memorial Library.)

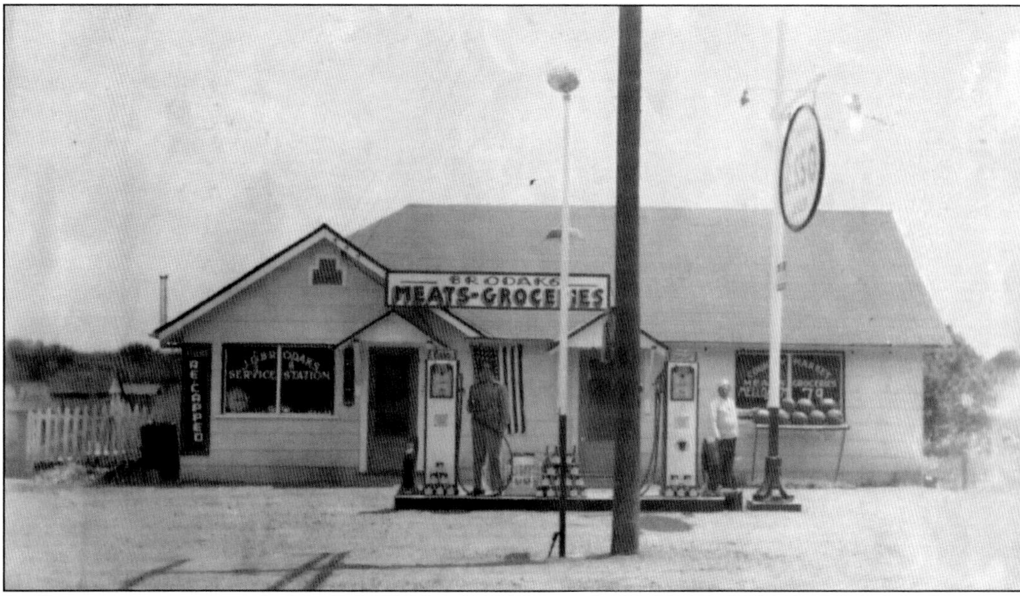

In 1942, Joseph and Valeria Brodak erected a large tent near the front of the 12-acre farm they purchased, which bordered on Route 88. Joseph worked in the coal mine and Valeria tended the garden and baked fresh bread to sell at their produce stand. In 1944, the stand was doing so well that Joseph found an old barn for sale, which he purchased and tore down, using the lumber to build the building seen here. (Courtesy of Flenniken Memorial Library.)

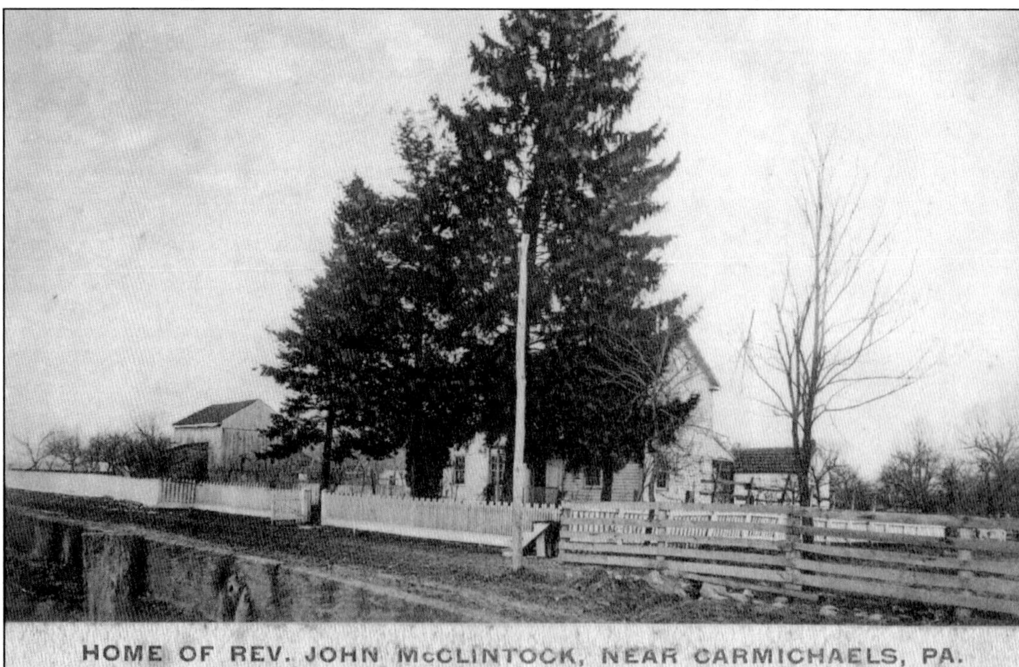

Rev. John McClintock served as pastor for the New Providence Presbyterian Churches for 50 years. Pictured here is the home of Rev. John McClintock, which was located halfway between the country church and the in-town church. In 1890, a book was published about Reverend McClintock and his 50 years of service. (Courtesy of Flenniken Memorial Library.)

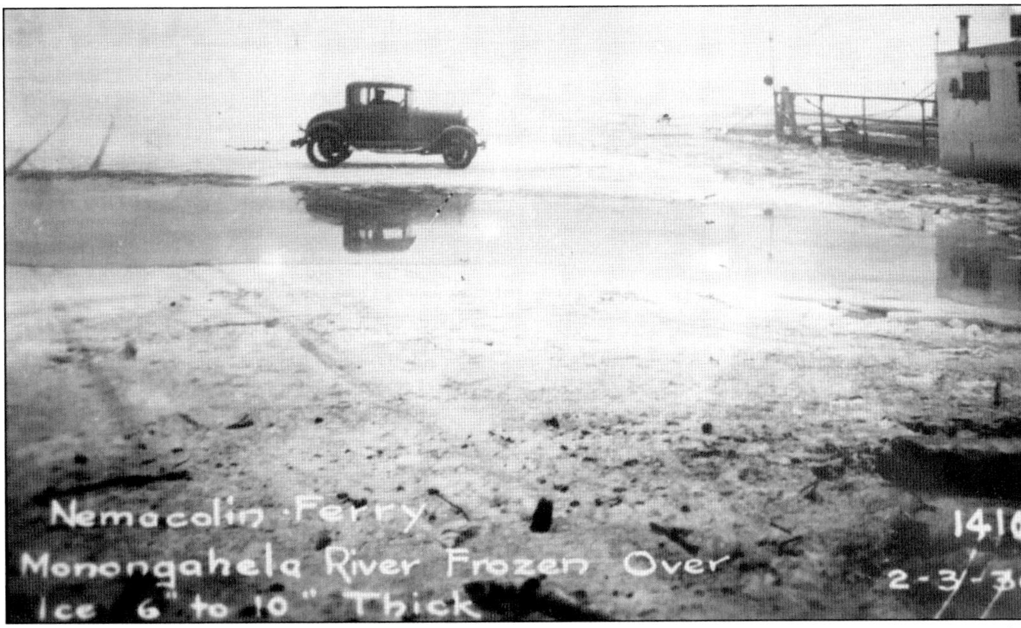

This picture, taken on February 3, 1936, shows the *Nemacolin* ferry stuck in the ice on the Monongahela River in Nemacolin. Charlie Klinger operated the ferry and, unable to get to work on the roads because of the snow and ice, drove his car across the river. The ice was reported to be 6 to 10 inches thick. (Courtesy of Brice and Linda Rush and the Robert Korcheck collection.)

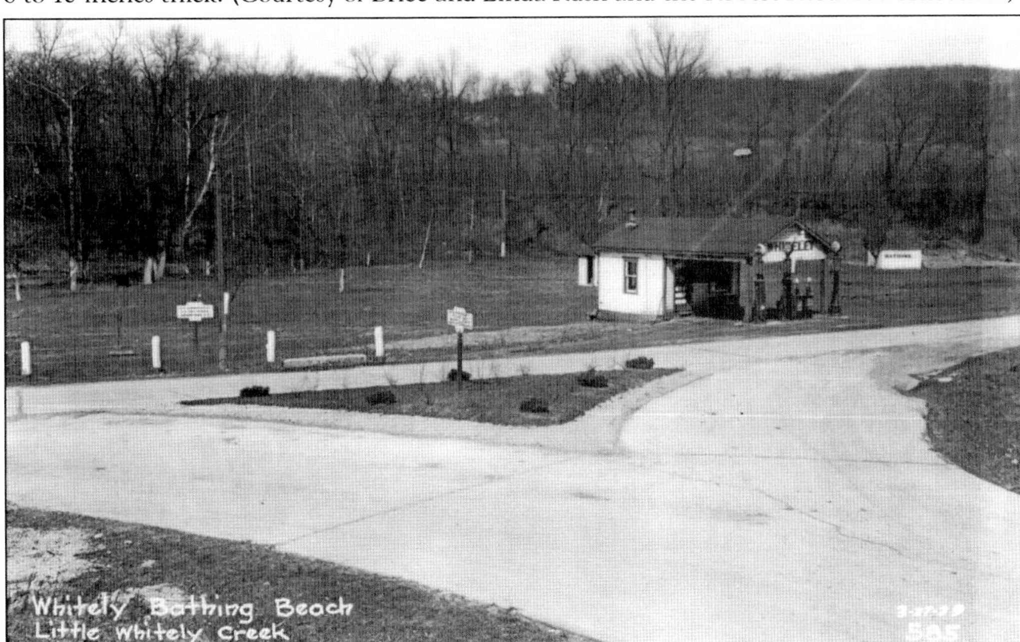

The Whiteley Bathing Beach and Whiteley Gas Station, once situated on Little Whiteley Creek and Route 21, are no longer in existence. Little Whiteley Creek passes through Kirby and Paisley and empties into the Monongahela River above Carmichaels. The beach was once a favorite place to swim. Driving through the Paisley intersection today, at 2605 East Roy Furman Highway is the Solomon car dealership. (Courtesy of Brice and Linda Rush.)

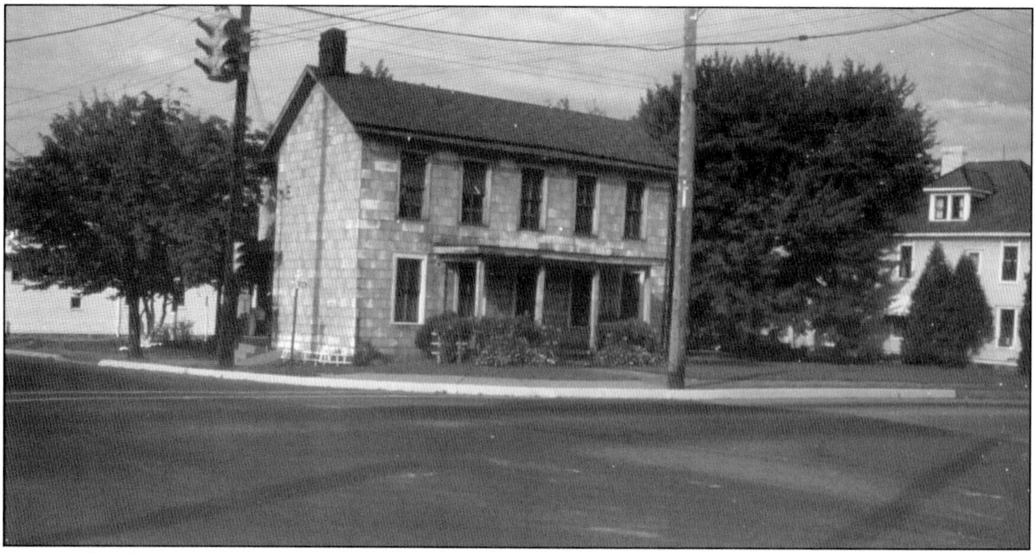

Pictured at the intersection of Vine and George Streets is what was once known as the Hathaway home, and to the right is the Laidley home. Both homes are no longer standing. They were torn down to erect a Circle K. (Courtesy of Flenniken Memorial Library.)

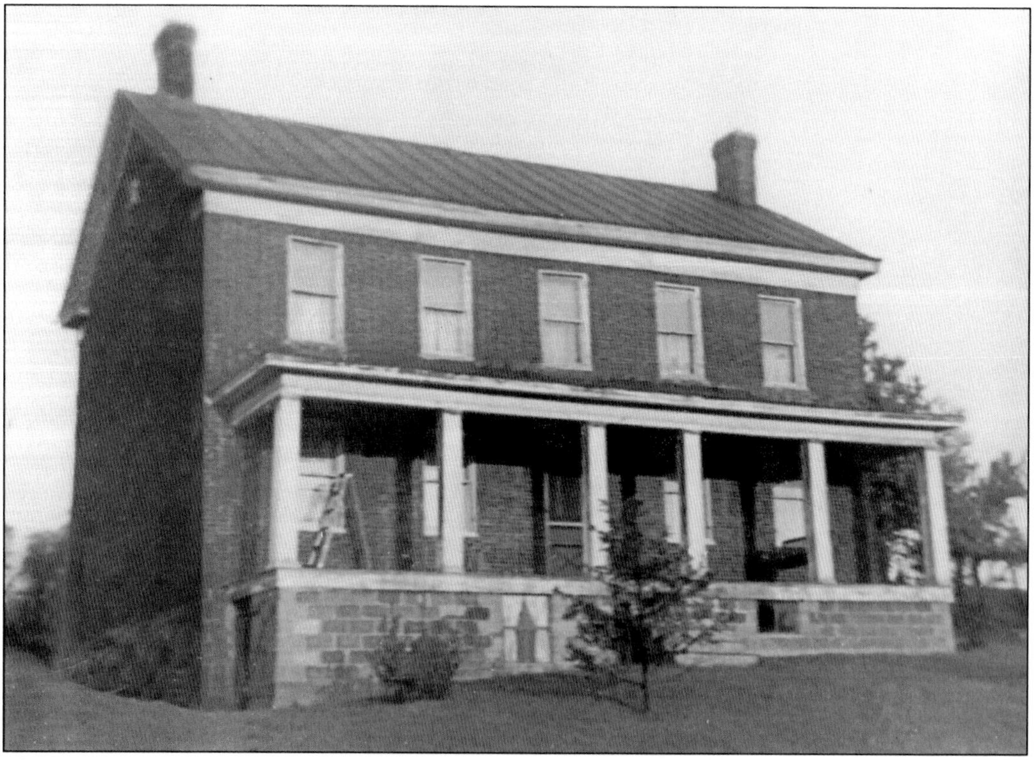

This is the brick house erected on the Armstrong homestead on Stringtown Road. The original cabin, which stood 200 feet east of this house, was built by John Armstrong in the late 1760s and was known as Fort Armstrong. The first church services held here, conducted by Rev. John McMillan, a Presbyterian minister, mark the beginning of the New Providence Presbyterian Church. (Courtesy of Dorothy Cunningham.)

This brick home was built in 1798 in Old Town along the banks of Muddy Creek and is still standing today. Folklore records that this home was once used as an armory. The first post office was located in a separate wooden structure, built in 1822, next to this house. The first postmaster was James Hughes. Chances are that this brick home was Hughes's residence. (Courtesy of Flenniken Memorial Library.)

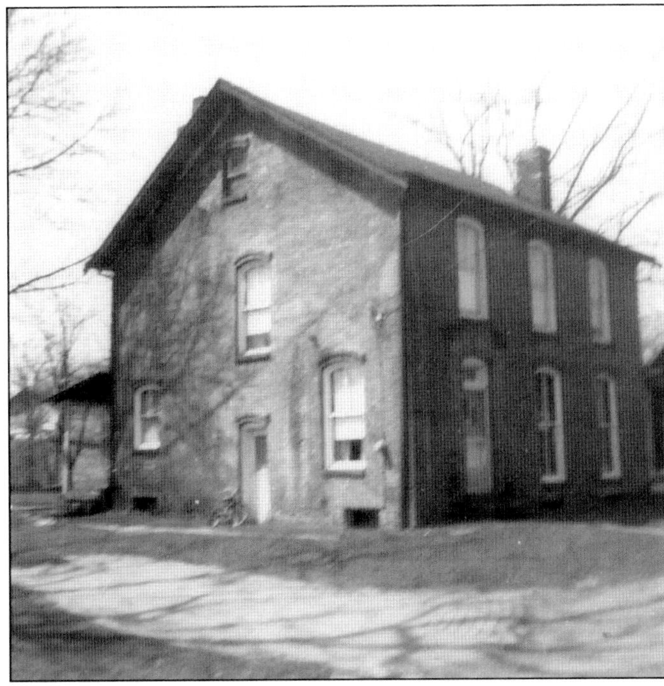

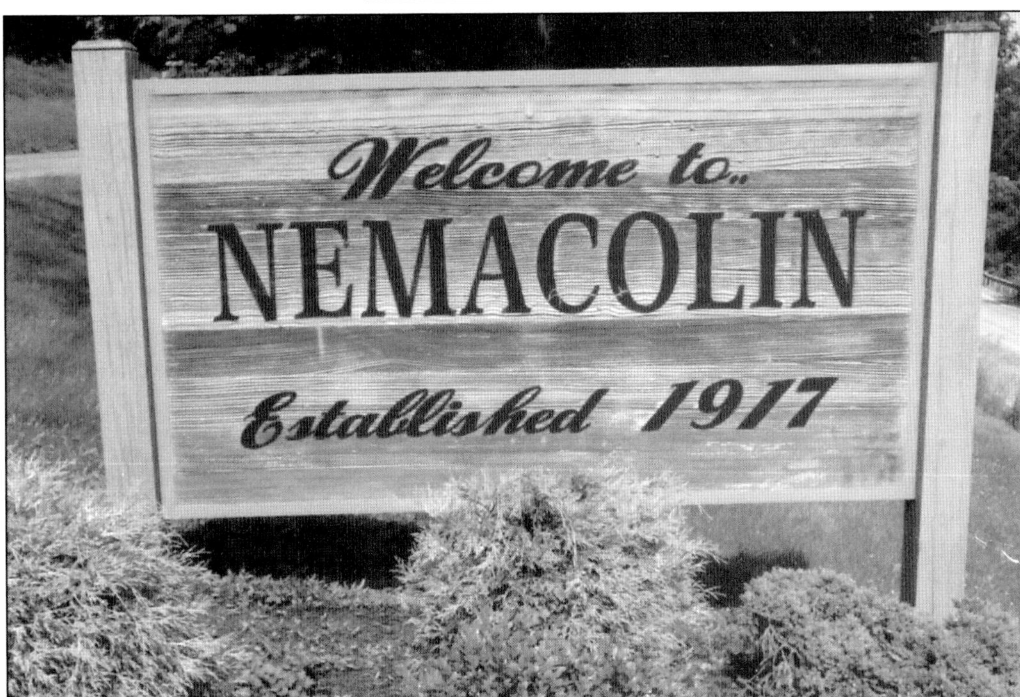

In 1917, the Youngstown Sheet and Tube Company thought this area was the perfect place to build a town. It was decided that the name of the town should have a meaning connected with local history. It was named after a Delaware Indian chief, Nemacolin, who had a village at what was known as Nemacolin Creek on the east side of the Monongahela River. The Indian pronunciation was "Nee–ma-ko-lin." (Courtesy of Brice and Linda Rush and the Robert Korcheck collection.)

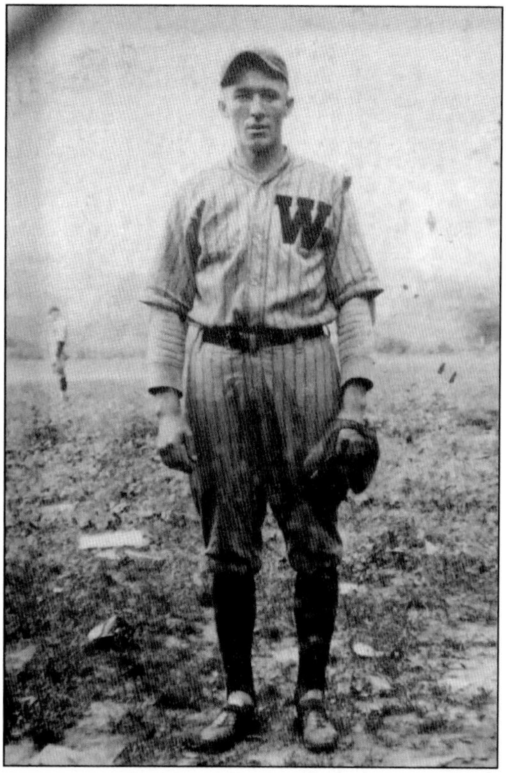

William McKinley Helmick, known in the world of baseball as "Chipper," was a left-handed pitcher who also played outfield. One newspaper article refers to Chipper as "one of the most brilliant all-around diamond athletes in this area." Chipper served during World War I, and while in LeMans, France, was awarded a bronze medal as an outstanding pitcher. After the war, he signed with different professional baseball teams. In 1926, he joined the Middle Atlantic League, where he was the first pitcher in the league to pitch a no-hit, no-run game. Chipper was one of many men from this area who played for professional sports teams. (Courtesy of Marcine Helmick McMinn.)

This early 1900s photograph shows a Vine Street house that once belonged to William Fred Burnette. (Courtesy of Mary Catherine Burnette Kirk.)

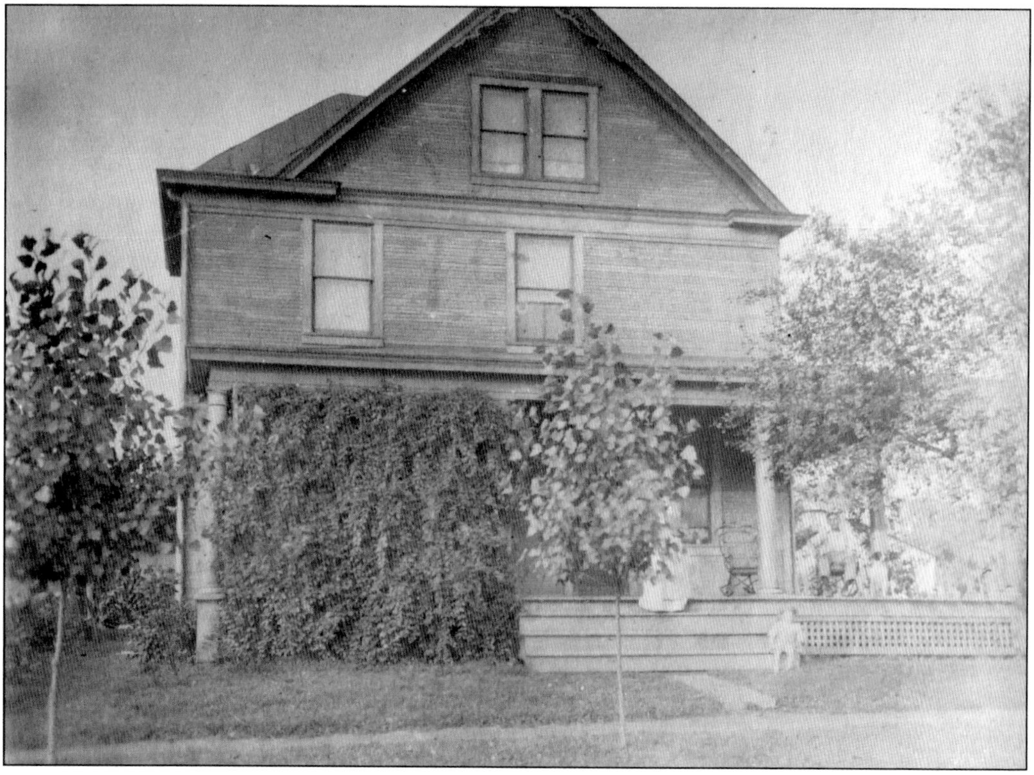

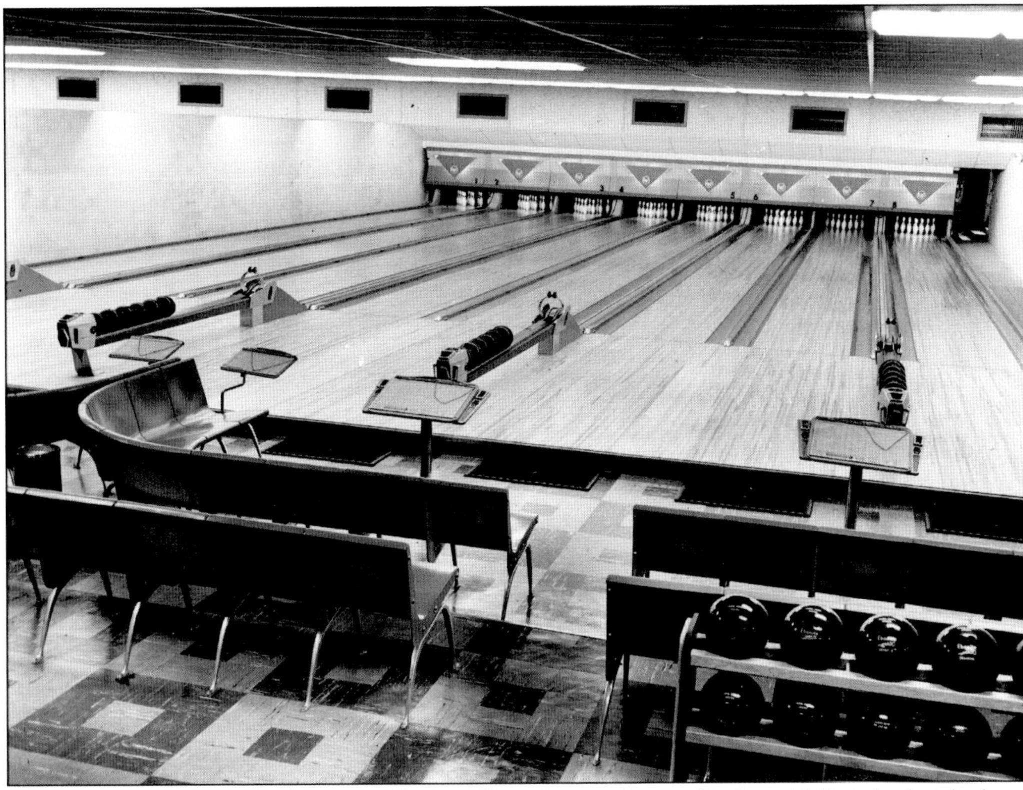

This is the interior of the bowling alley on West George Street. Built in 1960, it had eight lanes and a lunch counter. This was only one of the bowling alleys in town. In 1937, Dominick Christy Sr. established a duckpin bowling alley in the former Odd Fellows building. Werner Lund operated a bowling alley in the former Ross Theater. (Courtesy of Flenniken Memorial Library.)

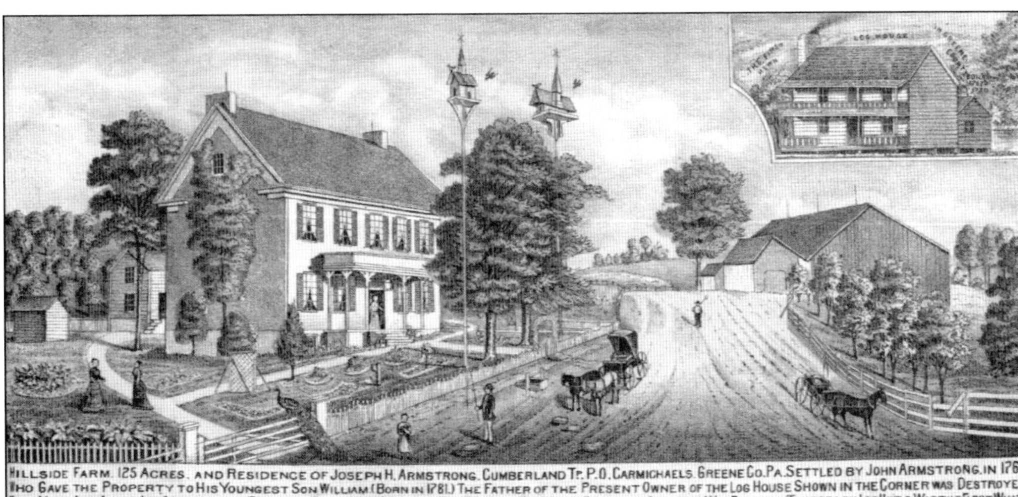

This lithograph depicts the Armstrong homestead, settled by John Armstrong. At upper right is the original log house, which was a fortified cabin that had portholes for firing muskets in the event of an Indian attack. (Courtesy of Flenniken Memorial Library.)

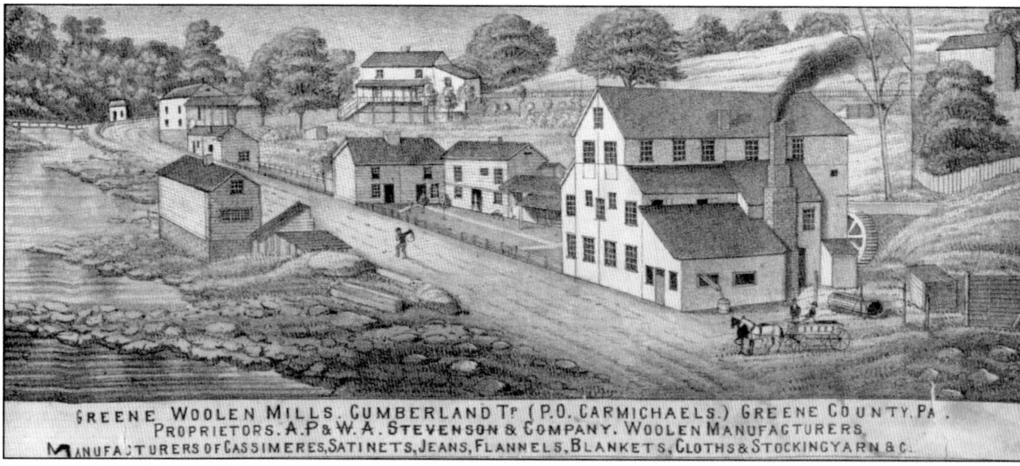

Greene Woolen Mills, pictured in this lithograph, was established by James Barnes and was located northeast of town on the banks of Muddy Creek. Barnes used waterpower to run the mill but also installed a steam engine, the first one to be used in Greene County, so that if there was a disruption in the flow of water, the production of the mill could continue. The mill produced blankets, flannels, yarn, and more. (Courtesy of Flenniken Memorial Library.)

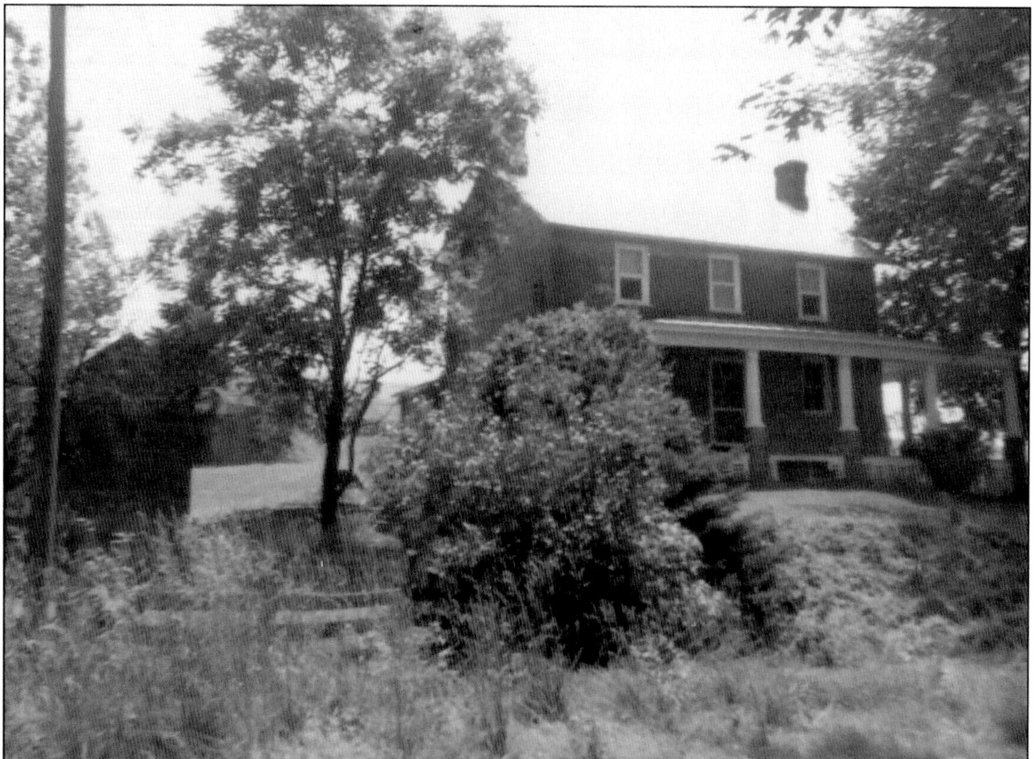

The property where this house is located was the site of the log home of Col. William Crawford. James Rea purchased a portion of the Crawford estate and moved the log home to an adjoining tract of land. The log house still stands and is listed in the National Register of Historic Places. In 1833, Rea built the brick house pictured here, which is still used as a private residence. (Courtesy of Carmichaels Area Historical Society.)

Six

Mining Communities

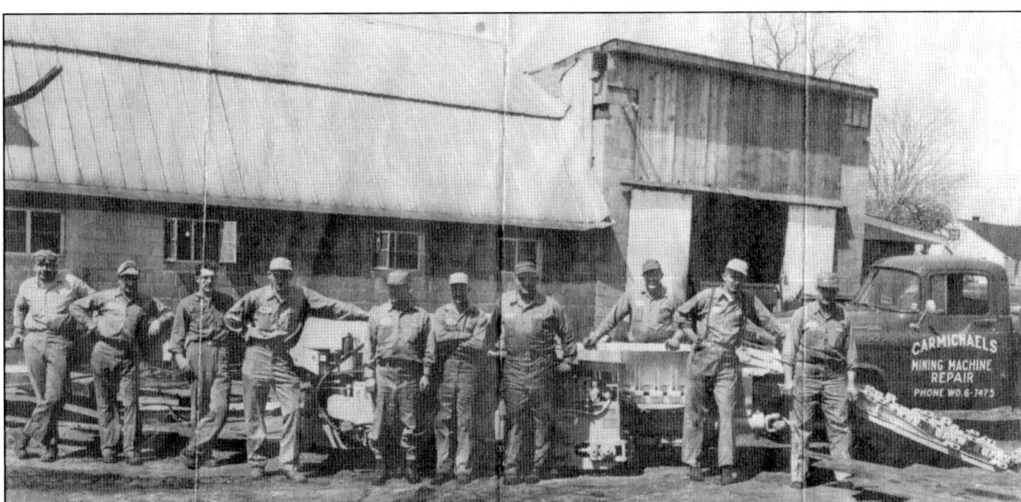

Pictured here are the members of the Carmichaels Mining Machine Repair Company. In 1957, the Crucible Mine shut down and five men, all former mechanics of the mine, decided to form a partnership for the purpose of doing repair work on mining machinery. They were Joseph Baker, Carl Osborne, Paul R. Roberts, Albert Kerr, and Daniel Swestyn. The company was in operation from 1957 to 1985, with a workforce of seven people. (Courtesy of Bill Groves.)

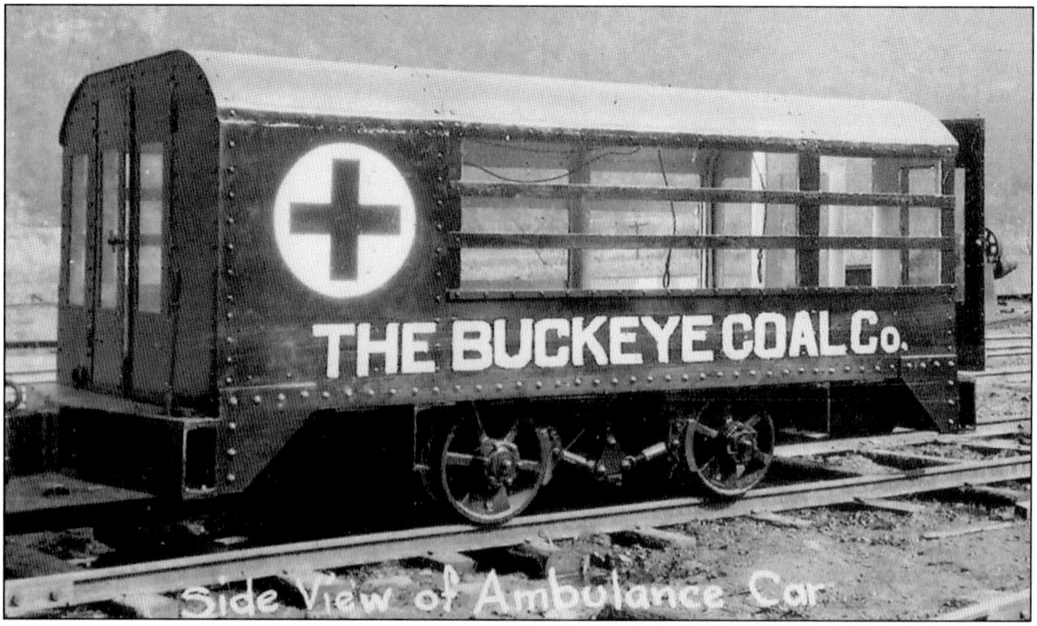

The Buckeye Coal Company ambulance traveled the rails into the coal mine to remove injured miners and rapidly administer aid. (Courtesy of Brice and Linda Rush and the Robert Korcheck collection.)

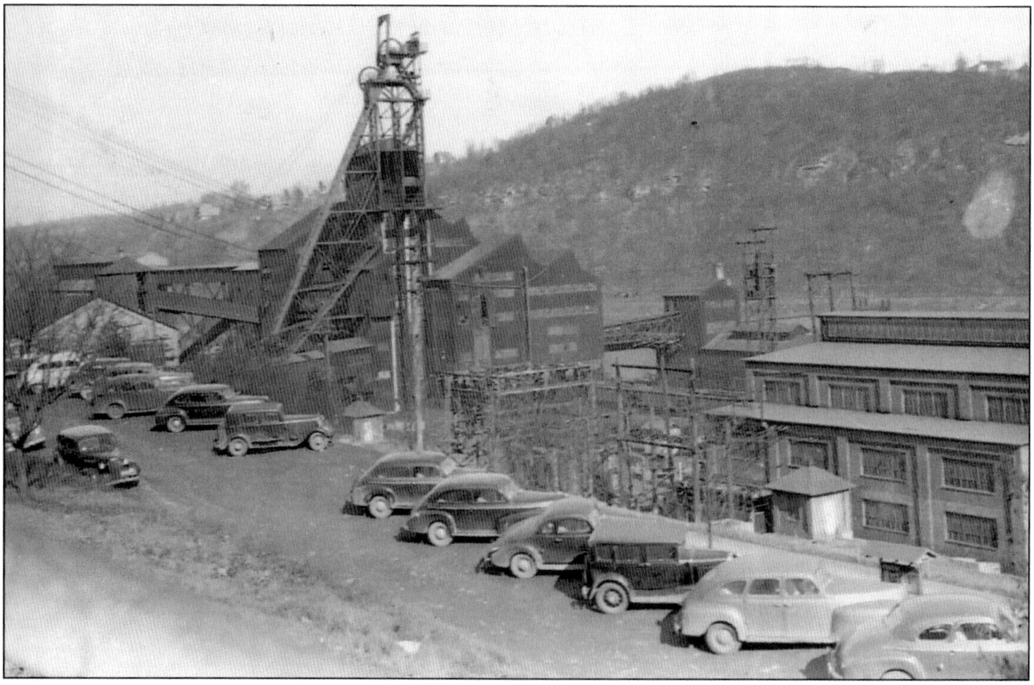
This is a view of the Nemacolin Mine, also known as the Buckeye Coal Company. Research by Robert Korcheck, Nemacolin resident and author, shows that coal was taken out of the mine in 1918. At that time, the Buckeye Coal Company employed 140 coal miners who brought out 23,573 tons of coal, which had to be cut by portable coal cutters. (Courtesy of Brice and Linda Rush and the Robert Korcheck collection.)

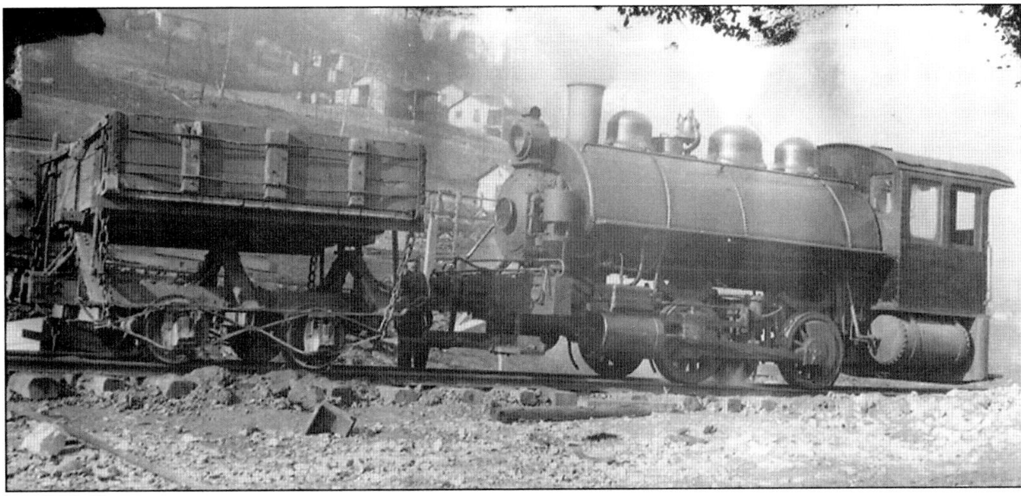

This is one of the locomotives used at the Nemacolin Mine. There were several different types of locomotives used over the years to gather coal. One was a storage battery locomotive, another was an explosion-proof cable-reel-gathering locomotive, and a third was a 13-ton Goodman trolley locomotive. This mine was the first in the United States to use the cable-reel-gathering locomotive in 1927. (Courtesy of Brice and Linda Rush and the Robert Korcheck collection.)

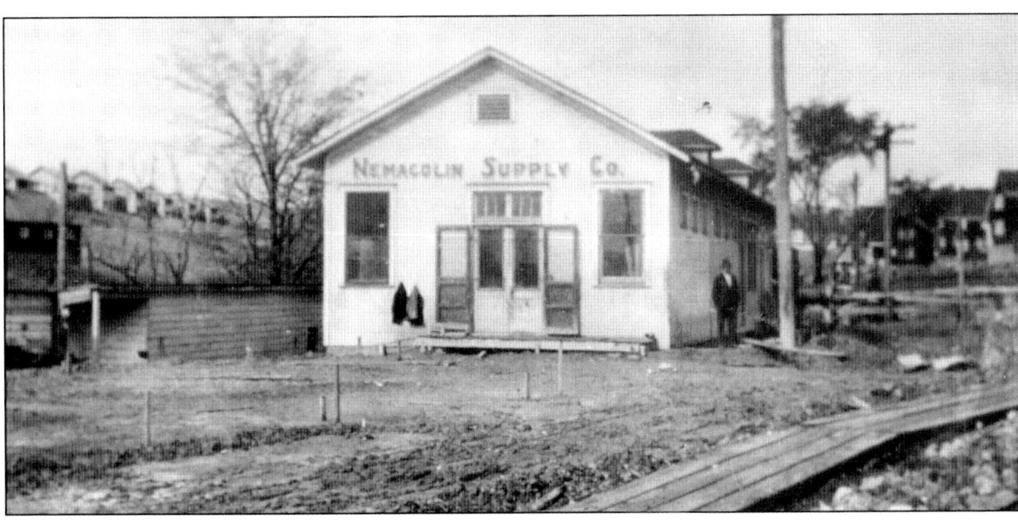

Pictured here is the Nemacolin Supply Company Store, built in January 1918. An addition to the store was completed on July 1 of that same year. After the addition was added, the first post office was opened inside the company store and remained in operation until 1961, when the building was destroyed by fire. (Courtesy of Brice and Linda Rush and the Robert Korcheck collection.)

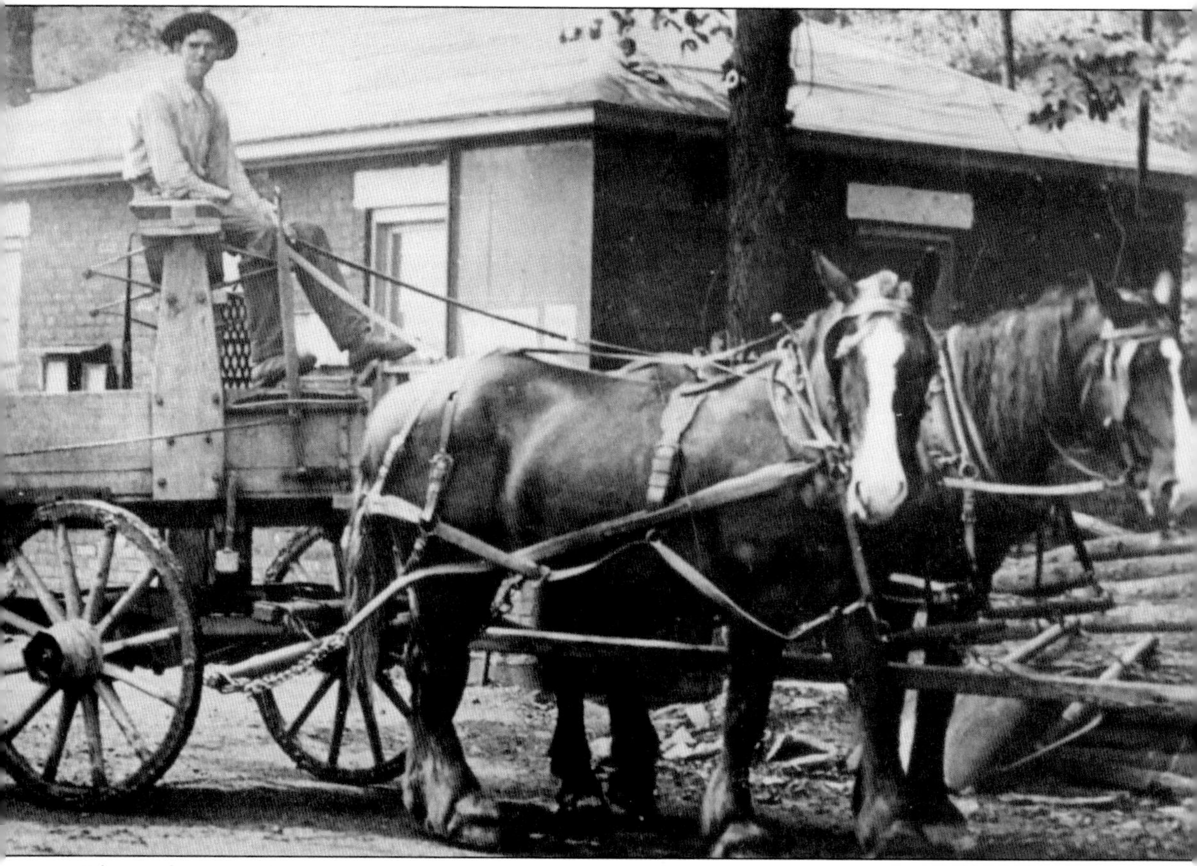

This early 1920s photograph of George Teagarden shows the Crucible Mine. The coal mine owned the company store that housed the post office, which opened in 1914. By 1960, the Crucible Coal Mine had closed. (Courtesy of Brice and Linda Rush.)

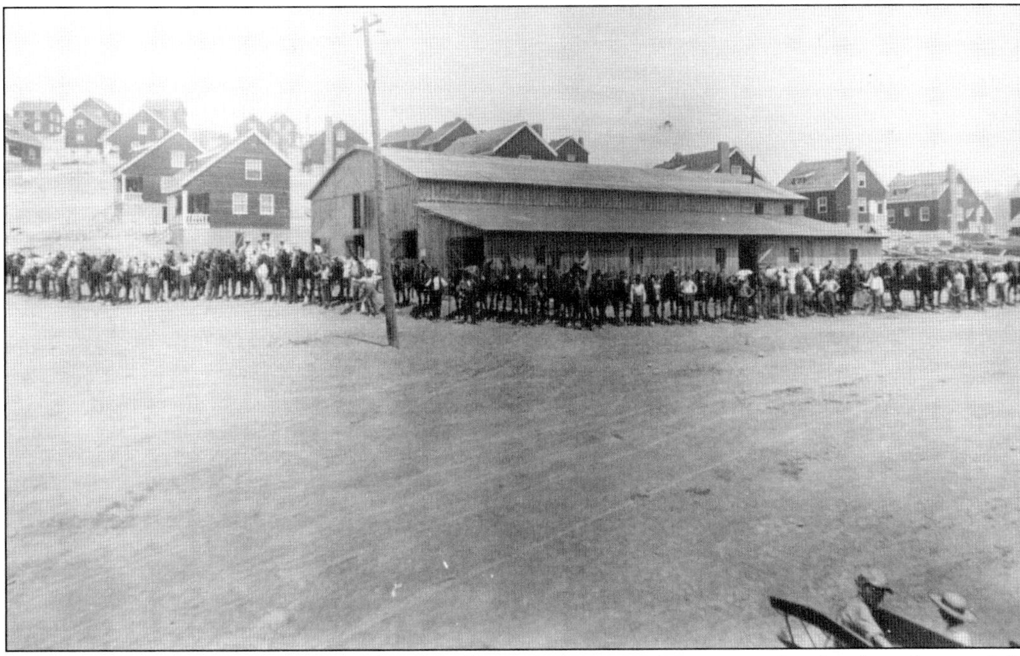

Pictured here are the original stables that housed the many horses used to haul coal out of the Nemacolin Mine. Behind the stables on the hill are the new homes built for the coal miners and their families. (Courtesy of Brice and Linda Rush and the Robert Korcheck collection.)

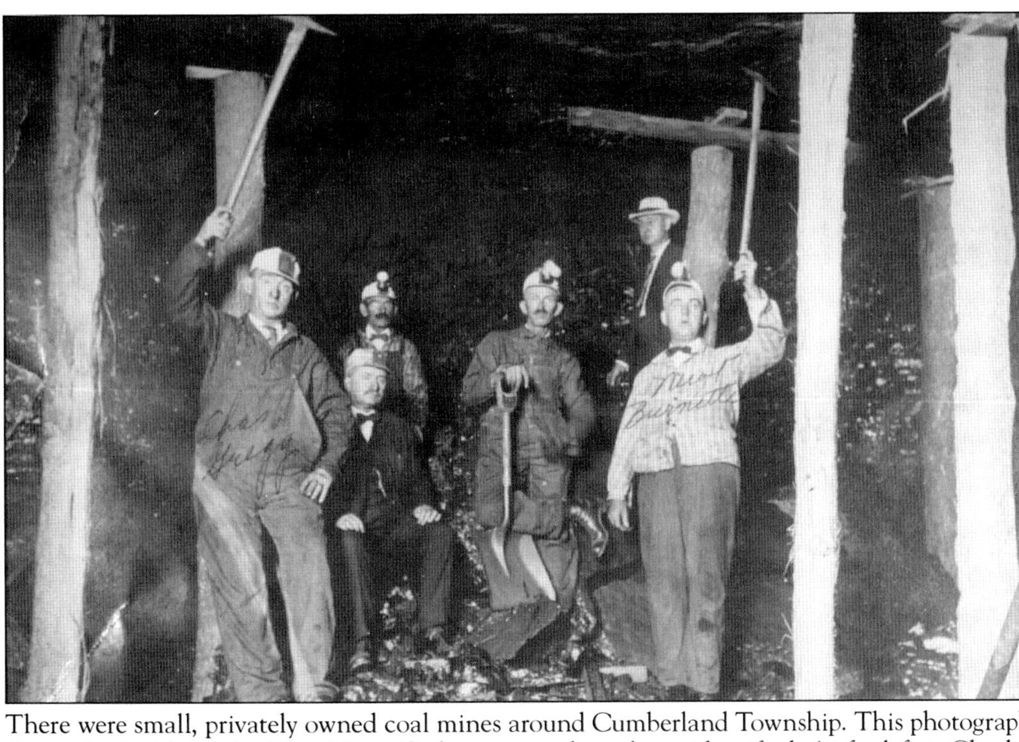

There were small, privately owned coal mines around Cumberland Township. This photograph shows the inside of the Hart Mine. Only two men have been identified. At far left is Charles Gregg, and at far right is Newton Burnette. (Courtesy of Charles "Bill" Hart.)

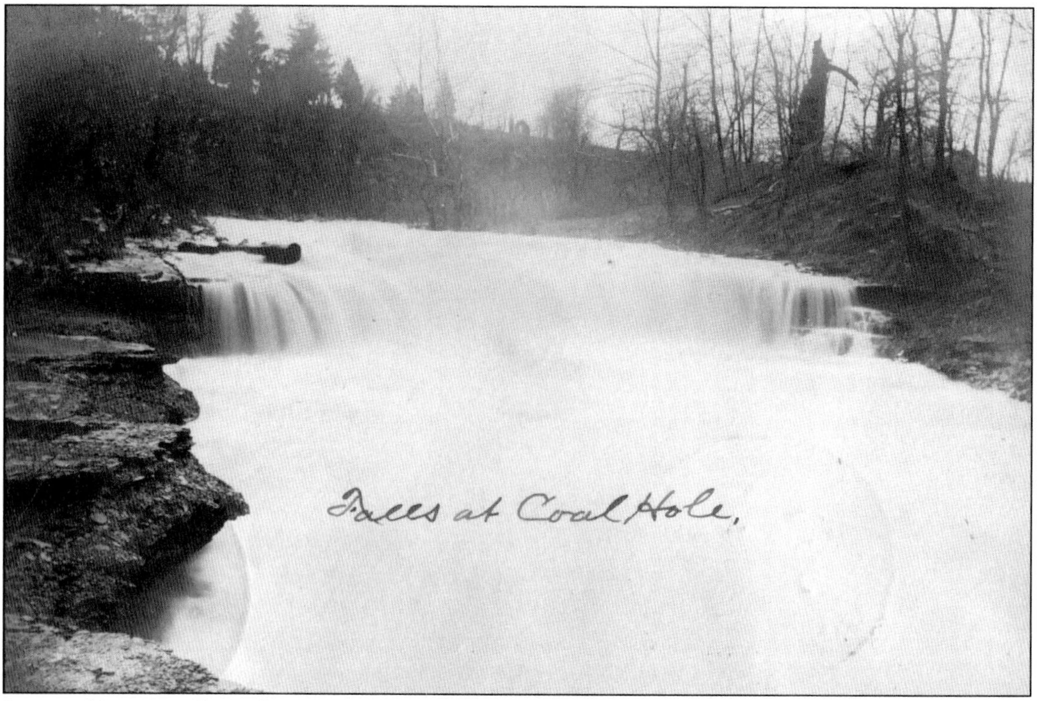

Pictured here are the Falls at Coal Hole prior to the construction of the dam restricting the flow of water. This area is now known as Laurel Point Falls, which is adjacent to the Laurel Point Cemetery. (Courtesy of Flenniken Memorial Library.)

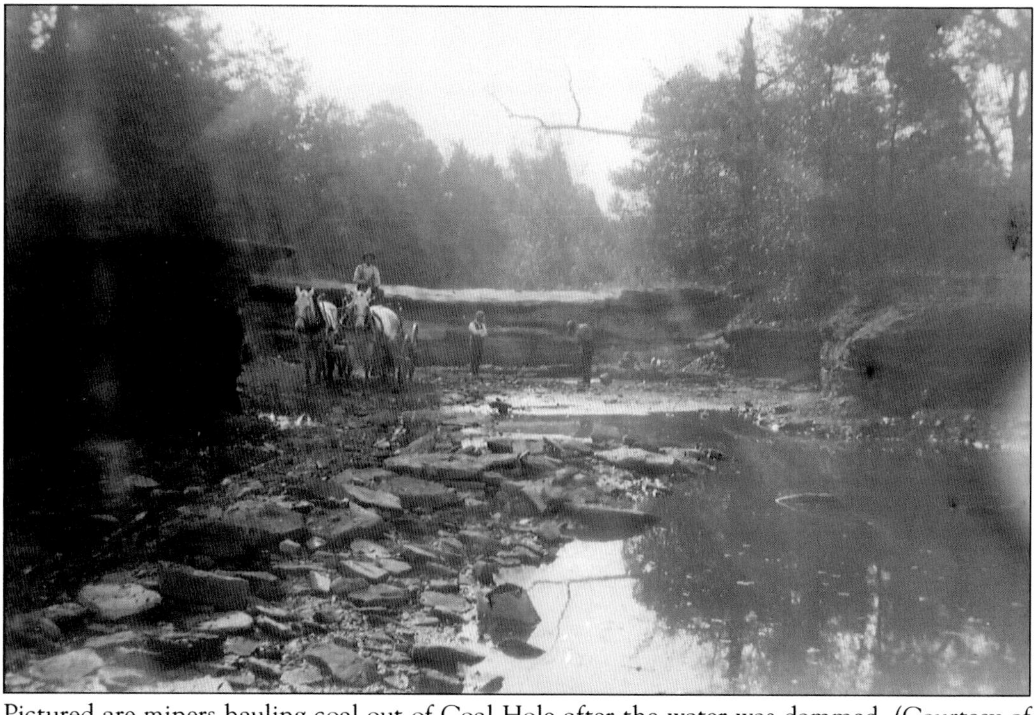

Pictured are miners hauling coal out of Coal Hole after the water was dammed. (Courtesy of Brice and Linda Rush.)

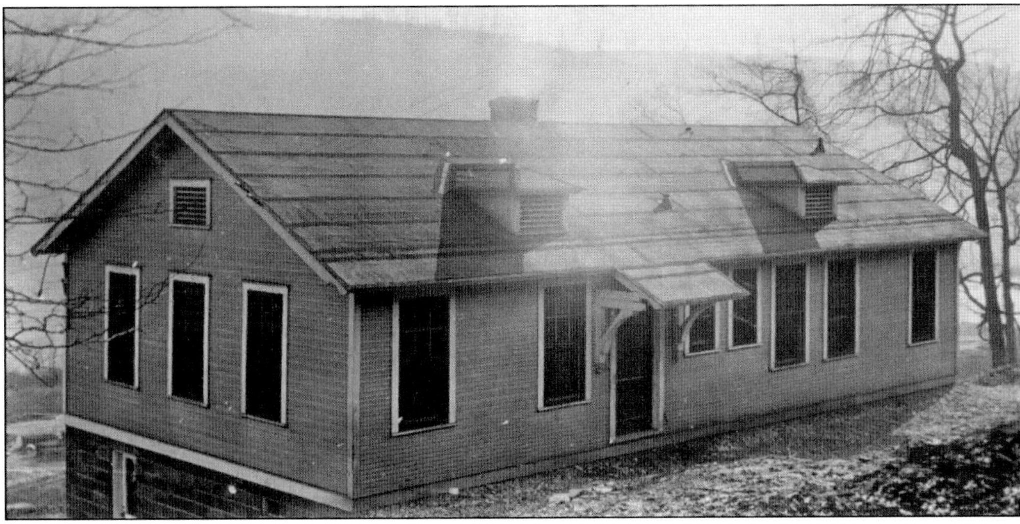

This was the emergency hospital in Nemacolin. This hospital was completed in May 1918 and was the first emergency hospital in Greene County. It was used until 1968. Two nurses who assisted the doctors were Margaret Young and Miss Warne, sister of elementary school teacher Lulu Warne. Nurse Warne resided in the hospital. (Courtesy of Brice and Linda Rush and the Robert Korcheck collection.)

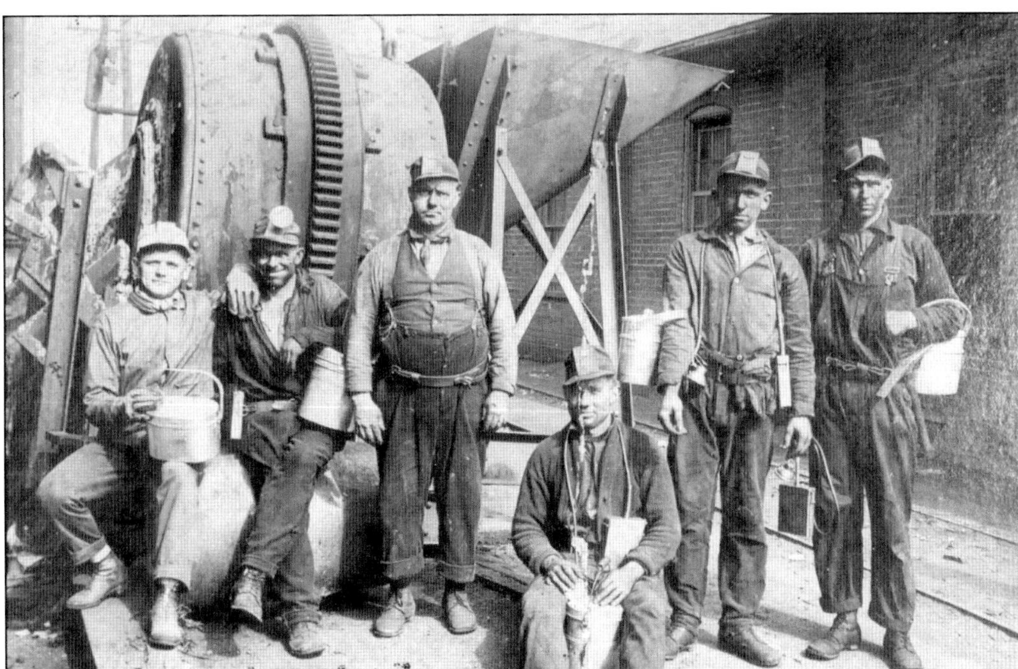

This group of coal miners worked at the Crucible Mine, which was opened in 1913 by Crucible Steel. At the peak of the mining industry in Crucible in 1953, the mine employed approximately 900 men and produced over one million tons of coal. The Crucible Mine closed in 1961. (Courtesy of Brice and Linda Rush.)

The No. 4 Shaft of the Buckeye Coal Company was built on Route 21 at the location known as the Bailey Schoolhouse. Prior to the construction of the shaft, the Bailey School once stood here, which dated to the late 1700s. Close to the school also stood a Baptist church, which was referred to as the Muddy Creek Church in the Goshen Baptist Church records. Rev. John Corbly preached at this church on alternating Sundays. Behind the church was a cemetery. The schoolhouse, church, and cemetery are no longer in existence. (Courtesy of Brice and Linda Rush and the Robert Korcheck collection.)

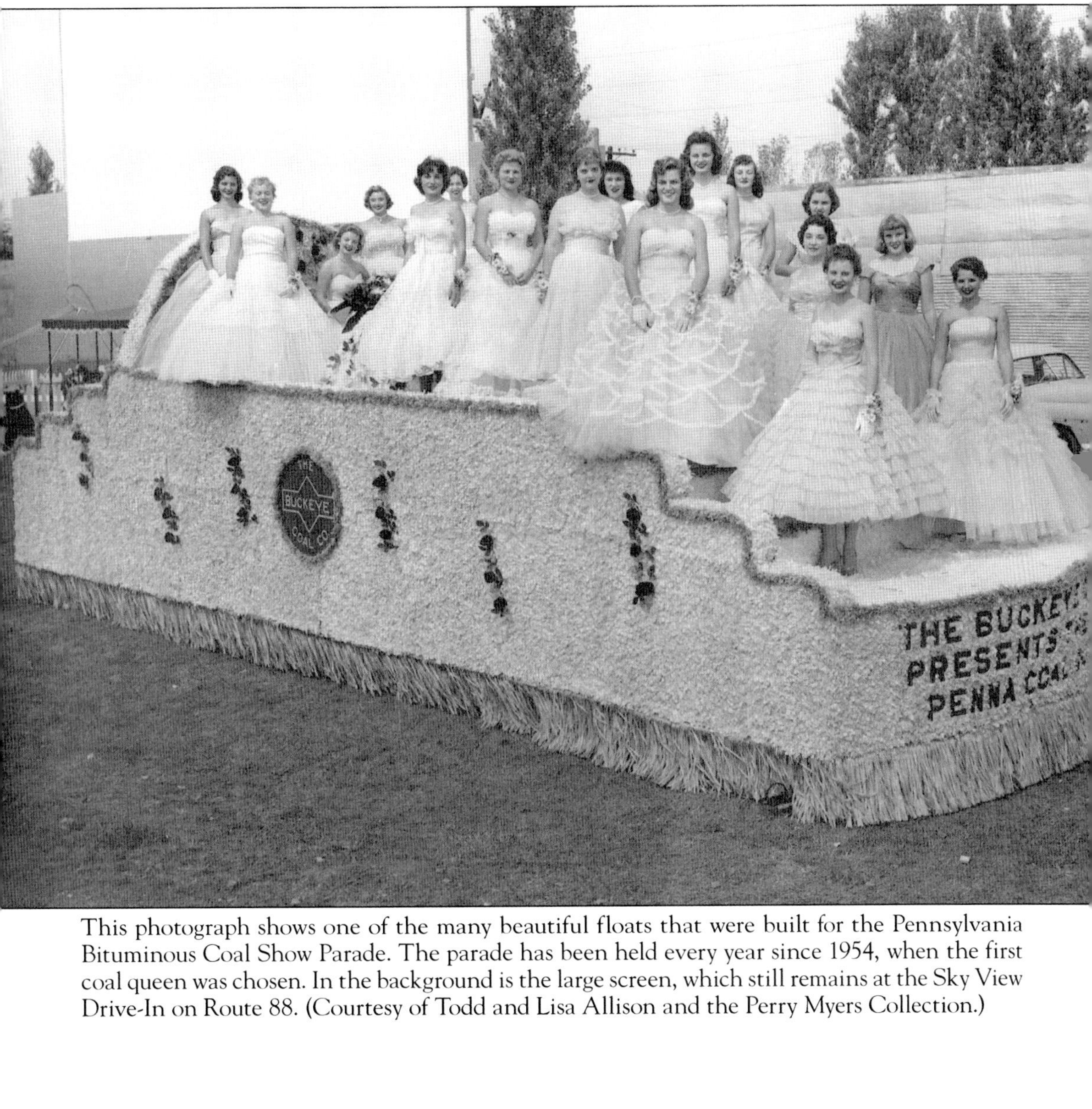

This photograph shows one of the many beautiful floats that were built for the Pennsylvania Bituminous Coal Show Parade. The parade has been held every year since 1954, when the first coal queen was chosen. In the background is the large screen, which still remains at the Sky View Drive-In on Route 88. (Courtesy of Todd and Lisa Allison and the Perry Myers Collection.)

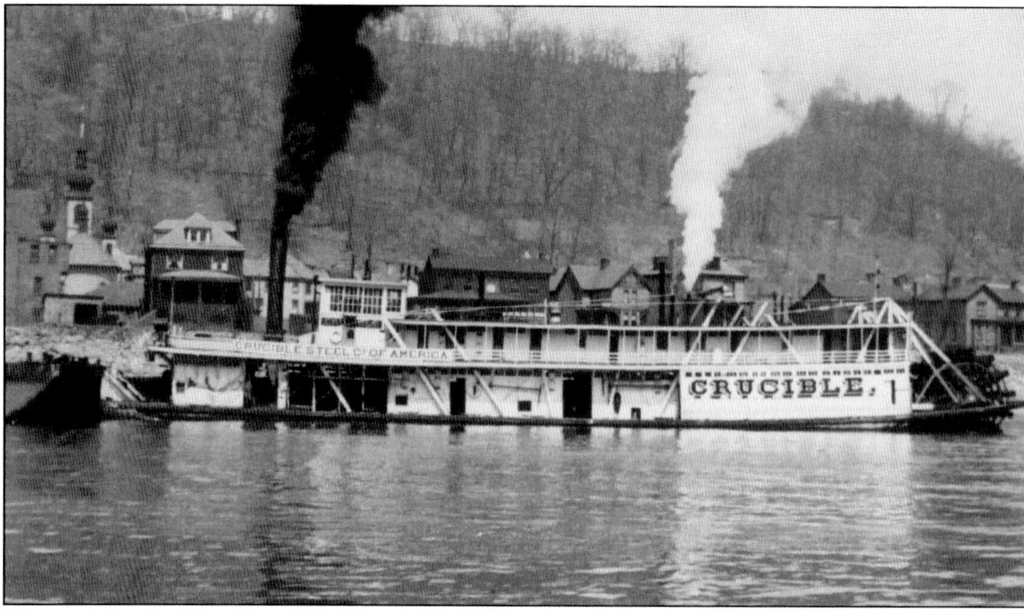

This paddlewheel boat was the property of the Crucible Steel Company of America and could be seen daily on the Monongahela River. (Courtesy of Brice and Linda Rush.)

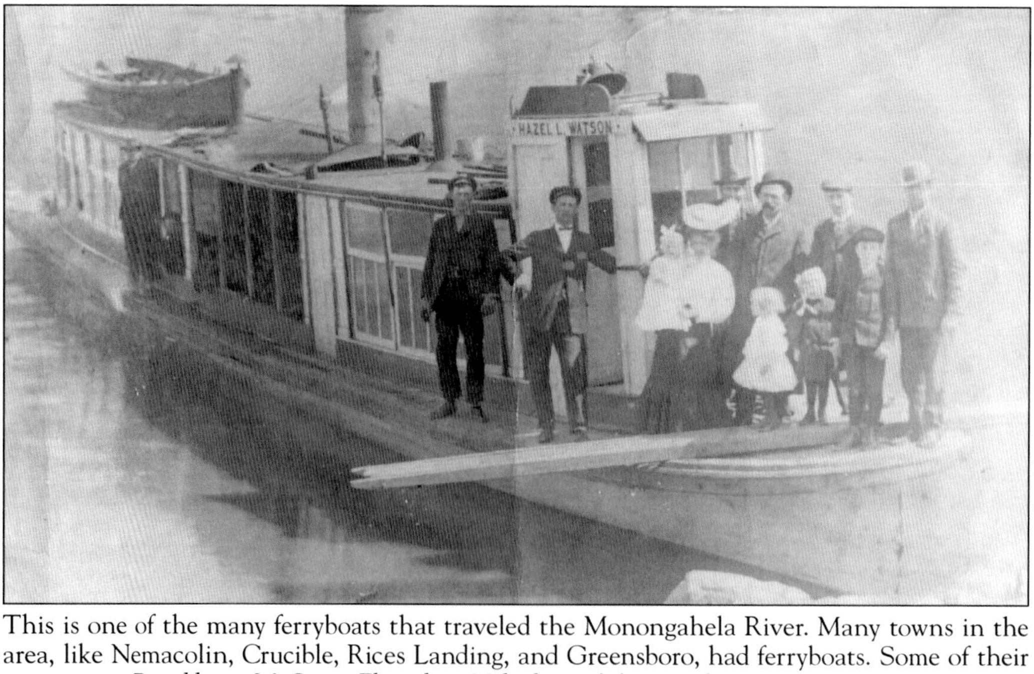

This is one of the many ferryboats that traveled the Monongahela River. Many towns in the area, like Nemacolin, Crucible, Rices Landing, and Greensboro, had ferryboats. Some of their names were *Republican*, *McCann*, *Flenniken*, *Nekoda*, and the *Hazel L. Watson*. (Courtesy of Joyce Fortney.)

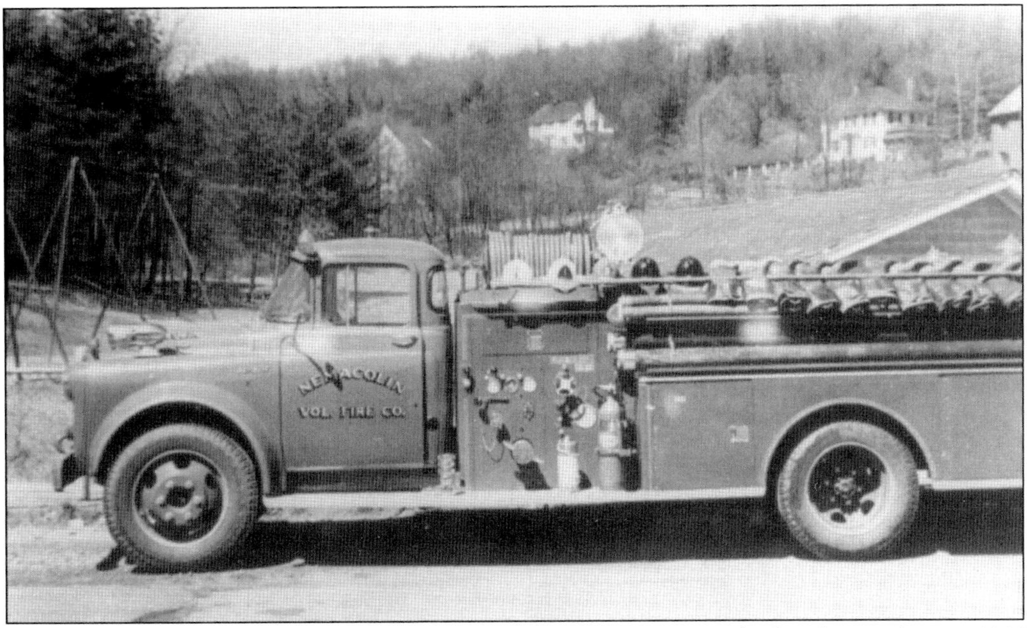

Shown here is one of the fire trucks of the Nemacolin Fire Company. The first fire truck was a 1916 Buick automobile that was rebuilt into a fire truck in 1923. The fire truck carried such items as 40-gallon acid soda tanks, two-gallon hand extinguishers, axes, hoses, lanterns, and a 30-foot extension ladder. This truck was used until 1934. The Nemacolin Volunteer Fire Department was organized in December 1946. (Courtesy of Brice and Linda Rush and the Robert Korcheck collection.)

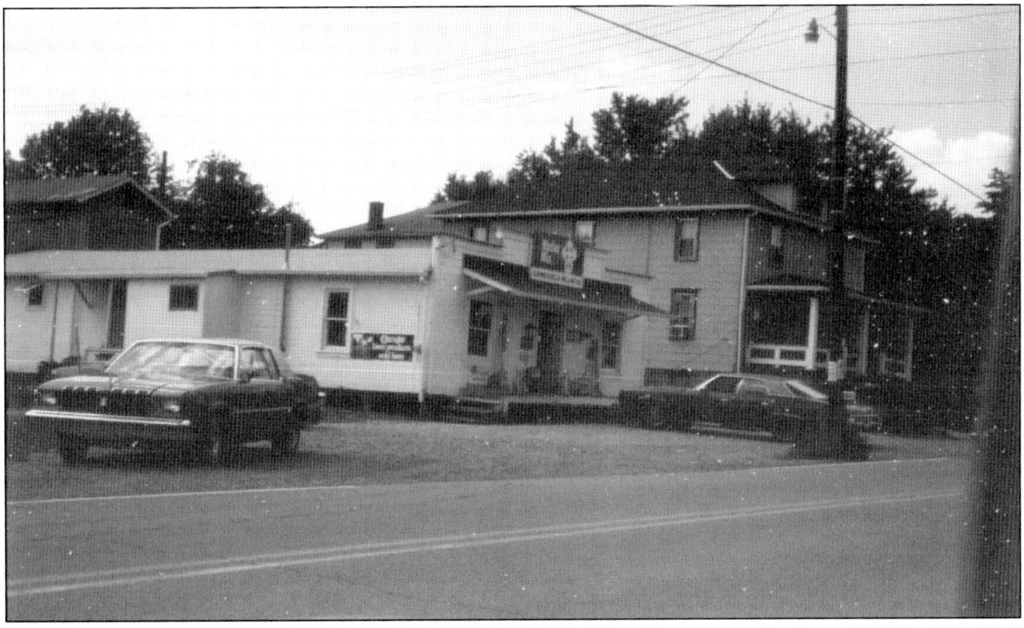

The Carmichaels Milling Company, located on South Vine Street, was built in 1928 by Playford W. Allison and Jonah Hart, who operated the feed mill until 1940. Michael and Blanche Yurick purchased the Carmichaels Milling Company in 1943, with the company still in operation in 1985. The mill ground corn, wheat, and all of kinds of animal feed. (Courtesy of Flenniken Memorial Library.)

Consistent with our mission to preserve history on a local level, this book was printed in South Carolina on American-made paper and manufactured entirely in the United States. Products carrying the accredited Forest Stewardship Council (FSC) label are printed on 100 percent FSC-certified paper.

MADE IN THE USA